1STUS Ed

10 =

FP/dj

FP

Peggy Burden

D1176287

l fn $20 - 35$

BALEIA ! BALEIA !

$BALEIA!$
$BALEIA!$

Whale Hunters of the Azores

Bernard Venables

ILLUSTRATED WITH PHOTOGRAPHS, MAPS,
AND DRAWINGS BY THE AUTHOR

ALFRED A. KNOPF  New York 1969

THIS IS A BORZOI BOOK

PUBLISHED BY ALFRED A. KNOPF, INC.

First American Edition
Copyright © 1968 by Bernard Venables. All rights reserved under
International and Pan-American Copyright Conventions. Published
in the United States by Alfred A. Knopf, Inc., New York, and in
England by The Bodley Head Ltd., London. Distributed by Random
House, Inc., New York. Manufactured in the United States of
America.

Library of Congress Catalog Card Number: 68–23959

To

HENRIQUE and JOSÉ (PETER) AZEVEDO

No traveler ever found better friends

Foreword

I C A M E in ignorance to the writing of this book. I knew little of the Azores (strange though that seems to me now) and less of their whaling. In the passage from ignorance to intimacy I had need of help; the warmth and generosity of its giving cannot be fitly recognized by mere formal acknowledgment. The help given made my book possible; it was, as much, an enrichment of life.

It was just luck that Dr. Alexandre Goulart should have been a native not only of the Azores, but of Horta itself, but I think he would have been no less wonderfully helpful had that not been so. He was, at that time, London Manager of TAP (Transportes Aeréos Portugueses), and he and TAP fathered me kindly to the farthest points of my exploring. Gratefully I thank them here for that.

And in Horta—what can I do but thank at large the whole of that warm community? Particularly, of course, I must thank those individuals whose consistent help overrode for me every difficulty. Henrique and "Peter" Azevedo, that forever-blessed pair, I have written of in the book, and no mere gesture of thanks can repay my debt to them. And indeed, where would I have been but for the quietly practical intercessions of Senhor Othon da Rosa Silveira or the fervent expositions of Senhor Tomas Alberto?

To Stanley Weston I owe unrestricted access to his immense scholarship about everything Azorean; Stanley Weston, so typical of a certain kind of Englishman to be found, little British islands by themselves, in countries over the earth. He, as English as any man could ever be, settled in Horta forty years, speaking the purest Portuguese, could answer me authoritatively on any question I could ask him about the Azores, from botany to ethnology.

And Senhor Norberto Frayão, who was forever in a fury of busyness, but was never so busy that he would not stop all to give me his help; to him, too, I owe my affection and my thanks. I must thank too Tourismo of Horta, whose protective umbrella was so great a help at all times.

To my several brief stays in Angra do Heroísmo, on Terceira, I owe not only the help of that most distinguished old man, Colonel Agostinho, but the deep pleasure and privilege of knowing him.

In describing the tools of the whalers I have drawn heavily upon Robert Clarke's authoritative monograph "Open Boat Whaling in the Azores," *Discovery Reports*, Vol. 26 (Cambridge, England: Cambridge University Press; 1954). I have transcribed various passages from it, having, while in Horta, checked them with authorities there, particularly Senhor Tomas Alberto. Robert Clarke's factual accuracy is indeed so exhaustively complete that his book must be a dominating background to the work of any who follow him.

October, 1967   BERNARD VENABLES

Illustrations

Photographs

(following page 50)

Technical Drawings

CORVO

FLORES

N

GRACIOSA

SÃO JORGE

FAYAL

PICO

TERCEIRA

SÃO MIGUEL

THE AZORES ARCHIPELAGO

SANTA MARIA

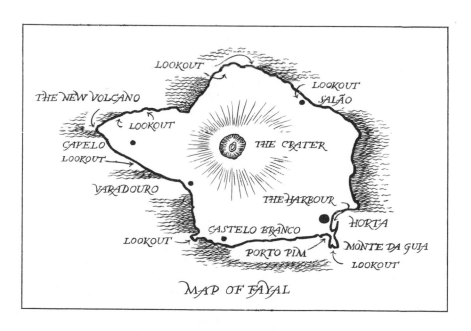

LOOKOUT

THE NEW VOLCANO

LOOKOUT

CAPELO

LOOKOUT

LOOKOUT

SALÃO

THE CRATER

VARADOURO

THE HARBOUR

CASTELO BRANCO

LOOKOUT

PORTO PIM

HORTA

MONTE DA GUIA

LOOKOUT

MAP OF FAYAL

BALEIA ! BALEIA !

CHAPTER

1

SO WILD a story enchanted the mind, and not the less so for its telling in the enclosed security of London. Its not quite imaginable evocation of raw perils had a remoteness that was not only of place but as much of time. Latter-twentieth-century man has become largely insulated against direct conflict with great beasts; he has long ceased to pit himself so carelessly. But this story had a tang of braver days—how are you to conceive a kind of men now who will go day by day so elementally against such naked danger?

In the Azores, so the story went, the sperm whale, that monstrous sea mammal, is hunted still by men in small open boats, boats without power, boats with only sails and oars and paddles. Their weapons, so puny for that quarry, are the hand harpoon and the hand lance. Just so, with no other aids, no protective mechanical modern means, they hunt that oceanic giant; they hunt it indeed as the old New England whalers did, with methods hardly changed at all. The only large difference is that the New Englanders hunted from boats lowered from whaleships; the Azoreans put off their boats from shore.

That was the story, and I fell into an obsession with it. What were the Azores? What was their nature, those mid-Atlantic islands? By what unique remoteness did they breed and sustain men and ways of such a kind? Of the Azores I realized that I knew almost nothing. Their inhabitants were Portuguese, and I had seen something of their kind—I had known the small dark seamen of Madeira and Continental Portugal, simple, hardy men. And, I recalled, I had heard that the Azores were beautiful, with the romantic turreted beauty that volcanic islands may have. But there hung about them, or so it seemed to me, a vapor of lonely ambiguity in that enormous openness of ocean. That there should come from that amorphous source so epic a story pricked a curiosity that became consuming.

Of the sperm whale I knew a little and, urged by my waxing preoccupation, soon knew more. How great indeed was this creature, I had wondered, how formidably big for so frail a means of hunting? Sixty feet and more an adult bull may be, with tail flukes more than twelve feet across, and with a third of that ponderous length made of the huge and queerly domed head. As I thought of the equation of that appalling bulk and those small boats I began to perceive that it might arise from something indigenous, perhaps even unique, in the nature of the islands and the islanders.

Obsessional curiosity may grow so far and then must be satisfied; my gleams of perception obscured rather than revealed. The teasing sense of enigma became compulsive; I must go to the Azores. I must see these men; I must see those lonely islands. In so seeing, I had begun to think, I might discover by what pregnant chance they were able to breed something so strangely out of period.

Great experience must not be come upon too quickly; there should be an interval of translation of context—and so much more so in this case, where not only had there to be an abandonment of one place for another, but of one time for another. My journey (it seemed) must be backward from the twentieth century. It was thus I thought it should be, but at once I found that there is no other way the Azores may be journeyed to; that was a first clue to their separateness. You cannot come any way but slowly to the Azores, or at least not to the farther islands.[1]

Modern modes of travel may whisk you so swiftly from place to place that the atmosphere, the texture of experience, may be partly vitiated; a place of departure should have time to dissolve, the destination come by degrees of revelation. To Santa Maria, the most easterly of the islands, I came quickly and easily enough, carried there with fine speed and luxury by TAP aircraft; from there the decline from modernity was to be steep, sense of time and distance to seep out of consciousness. I was going to Fayal, and even in Santa Maria I was to feel that Fayal was remote.

But, as though transition should not be too abrupt, the journey beyond Santa Maria was at first still by air, by air still but by the little Dakota aircraft of SATA which plies between the more easterly of the islands. After the elegant monsters of TAP, it seemed (so do we become conditioned) like one of those happy little blackened puffing trains by which we used to make our local rural journeys. Santa Maria airport, a small impingement of outer-world sophistication, was left behind; the aerial amble of the little plane came to São Miguel to land on an airfield that is indeed a field. We came to our gentle landing through a swish of long

[1] *But change will come even to the Azores. Air transport is to reach out to the farthest islands, and may have begun to do so when this book is published.*

grass. Then, after a shooing of the cows for the take-off run, on to Terceira, where, at the airport, there was a momentary flurry of modernity because it is also a minor U.S. airbase; but that was a last small gesture.

Now the large world, all its urgency, had gone; I was on the narrow road to Angra do Heroísmo, the island's major (indeed only) town. I was in the Azores now and must go at the Azorean pace, which does not acknowledge urgency. Two days must be spent in Angra before a little ship could take me through the islands to Fayal—to Fayal, so much nearer now but seeming more intangibly remote than it had in London. Two days, two hours, two weeks? My cognizance of time was already weakened, and I was only a few minutes on the road to Angra; in those minutes the airport had melted into the unreality of Lisbon, London, all else that had been left.

It was an inconstant road, running to the heave and toss of the volcanic terrain, and, as I followed its loops and drops and sharp ascents, the idea returned and grew that in the islands there might be an indigenous ferment of chance that bred men of a certain kind. The thought was forming that the presence of whales was ancillary to the nature of these men rather than being their main motivation. I had the sense, elusive as yet, below conscious level, of some sort of simmering contradiction; I perceived an oddity of contrast though, so far, it was no more than first and only intangible impression. A simplicity, an ingenuous gaiety of life were apparent; but no less so was an immediate feeling of its eruptive context.

Little fields were about the road, little fields stolen from the abrupt climb of the land, and each bore its tiny crop of blue lupine or crimson clover fodder, and each was circumscribed within its terracing walls of boulders. But under the walls, clambering over them, rioting on the banks, was such a queer companionship of plants that in the groping trend of my thought they seemed to have a significance. There were, I could have sworn, familiar English wild flowers, such English meadow innocents as demure mauve mallows, and hawkweed; then abruptly there were great succulent stands of cactus and aloe with bold flares of blossom, extravagant tumbles of ipomoea, scarlet hibiscus. In the little fields, in the small gardens by the color-washed houses, there was a beguiling tranquillity, but the sense was there of a bare containment of an eruptive smolder.

I turned my eyes to the heights, and no innocuous hills were these, no peaceful foldings of strata; each peak, each soaring eminence was a volcano. The realization came suddenly of the hot upthrusting origins of the islands, and I saw that the sharp tilt of rocky flanks where the vines flourished so peacefully were old lava flows. The bouldery walls that clutched the little strips of cultivation from the rugged sheer were superficial reminders of Ireland, but these stones were porous volcanic rock, just as it had cooled, not limestone.

There were villages on the road, and when the way dropped down into them the whispering sense of the molten thrust abated. How could any such consciousness continue in villages so gaily enchanting? In their Portuguese fashion they had a spontaneous architectural sense, a happy decorativeness as natural an outflowing as speech. The buildings, white or pink or green, had a delighting little fancifulness of decoration, never inappropriate. There was a church, white and low, rather squat in its engaging fashion, with stout twin towers. Raised from the center of its white wall was a sea-blue plaque. It read 1865. I looked at its innocent perfection and thought of the monstrous architecture that that period saw in England and America.

As the villages were, so, in its larger way, was Angra, a little town of such a cool and pretty comeliness, so clean and lightly beautiful, coming with such ingenuous elegance down the falling slopes to the harbor, that its volcanic hinterland could be forgotten. Its streets were narrow, as Portuguese streets are, with patterned pavements, black and white, against the guileless charm of the façades, opening into small squares in a shade of palm and acacia. It was a town to lull time and purpose, to soothe away determinations. But my mind was on Fayal, on its whalers; the obsession stayed even in this tranquillity. And, now, *Espirito Santo* was in the harbor, that little ship that was to take me through the islands at last to Fayal.

"Ship" it must be called in the absence of a more definitive word; but how small a ship, how hardly adequate a ship, no bigger than the tuna boats with whom she lay against the quay. I made my inspection of her dubiously, took my ticket, and took to heart my instructions.

"Be there in good time," they said; "She sails at seven, at seven promptly. Don't be late."

And I, up at half-past five, was there in good time, at half-past six, and so were a great many other people, more people, as I could see, than could possibly go aboard that sea bantam. They are here out of curiosity, I thought, or to see off friends; but go aboard they did, all of them, inexplicably, wonderfully, they and as mixed a jumble of cargo as ever a ship carried. The cow went aboard by belly-sling, and the oddly useless-looking pile of timber followed her into the hold, as did the pots and baskets and bicycles and crates and bundles of clothes and the old-fashioned mangle, and after that the passengers. *Espirito Santo* rose and fell on the swell, the short rough wooden stepladder was given an impromptu lashing, and, each in turn, the passengers made the adventurous boarding, and I took careful note of the manner.of it as I waited. Stand poised on the quay's edge, wait until the rise of the surge brought the gunwale within three feet below, then half-fall, half-aim a foot at the ladder's top rung, then be caught by the two crew members either side of the ladder. So went those before me, old black-shrouded peasant women, mothers and children, cripples and crutches, and then I was aboard with a curious aerial ease.

This was the lower deck, already a close press of passengers in its little confinement, and I made the nearly vertical ascent of the companionway, with its bare shoulders' width at the top, to the upper deck. I staked a claim there, securing a purchase by shoulder blade against the corner of the tiny deckhouse with its four berths.

We did not sail at seven; a little after half-past seven the small Diesel funnel, at my elbow as I now realized, burst into a staccato thunder that expunged all other sound. The voyage had started, an odyssey within a day, a passage out of present, out of time. We cleared the harbor, met the swell, and I lurched against the funnel to find it had become too hot to touch.

It was a kindly sea, with a mild and oily swell; but to be a poor sailor has no qualifications. Even the Diesel thunder at my elbow could not entirely muffle the chorus of illness that fell upon the ship, and the fair sea wind spread among us impartially the not quite atomized detritus. Time again took dimension—twelve hours more of this, I thought, and edged around behind the deckhouse where perhaps the wind's spread of illness might be mitigated. For about two hours I contemplated that glum prospect, and then we came to our first place of call at the eastern end of São Jorge; there, most providentially, the majority of passengers went ashore.

To say they "went ashore" suggests a simplicity in so

doing, but Azorean coasts are wild; the dizzy fall of precipice goes sheer to the breakers. The quay at this place is the merest notch in a jagged elbow of cliff, a tiny shelf of stability in so much boil of sea and ferocity of rock. Approaching it, lurching on the swell that towered and broke, I could see no way that *Espirito Santo* could be persuaded into manageability against the quay. But persuaded she was, edged and coaxed until she nudged gently to her mooring,

and I saw that just against the quay there was a small area of placidity, hardly more than the size of the ship. There she was now, tied up and lifting and falling in her precarious haven, and the people were going ashore with the adroitness that islanders have. The shuffling old women in their peasant black, balanced on the gunwale by two crewmen, showed a certainty of foot at the moment the swell lifted to the quay's level.

The quay was crowded, it and the terraces of road that hairpinned down the face of the precipice; the dark faces peered and shouted and called greetings. In the thronging jostle the oncoming cargo waited—balks of timber, a black brass-knobbed bed, basketed wine bottles, two cows and four calves, sad-eyed and apprehensive. As the cattle swung aboard in the belly-sling, I looked at the sea-carved sheer of the precipice, 700 feet at a guess, striped with layers of harsh gray lava and red volcanic refuse.

Now the ship's siren sounded, a startling blast for that small craft; the little quay receded. There was room on the upper deck now, room to sprawl a little, blink at the sun as *Espirito Santo* crept westward under the towering coast of São Jorge. Time had dissolved again, no past, no future, an eternal present, a dream; the sense of an odyssey recurred, with Fayal perpetually insubstantial and unreached. The long coast passed slowly on our beam, and I felt the vague memory of all the legends told of island voyages, of Hesperides, of Atlantis. Common reality had lost meaning, with the sea as deeply blue as liquid pigment and the wild coast soaring to a fantasy of summits. Down the long vista of the island there was pile upon pile of peaks, a crenelation of volcanoes above the dizzy scarp of precipice. Could there be, I wondered, a more complete substantiation of imagined dreams of romantic islands, so pinnacled, so rich with growth, so laced with silky ravels of waterfall? To such a place, surely, I must come, so far from commoner contexts, to bring to reality something with so distant a ring of legend as this whaling.

To be born of that eruptive upthrust from the sea *must* make an ingredient of character not found in more mundane origins; some fiery seed of it *must* be implanted. Perhaps there was a sign in the colonization of the wild hangs of cliff and lava slope, like seabirds on a crag; I could see the continuation of small houses on eyrie ledges, the road that clung and hairpinned, the tiny terraced fields from sea to towering edges. People who live in such precipitous places usually have a capacity for using every last inch of cultivable land, but for these Portuguese islanders it was ingenious and daring. It had a verve, almost an impertinence, in that wildly intractable place.

Espirito Santo had its places of call along the coast,

sometimes mere jetties wrought into a rock pile under the cliff or in the jagged tail of a lava flow, served by a road that came precariously from the hinterland. To these footholds in the lash of sea a boat was lowered and sent tittuping over the swell to land its passengers and freight; each time I watched with uneasy speculation, fearing lest it be smashed against the stones. But, each time, I saw the casual mastery of its handling; I saw that, fine seamen as these islanders are, above all they are superb boatmen. The boat was edged in, poised on the swell, just nodded alongside; passengers and goods were landed, new passengers taken aboard.

At the villages and little towns huddled within the plunge of the lava slopes, *Espirito Santo* tied up at the quay, but before each landing there was forewarning, a rising excitement, because each was a return for someone aboard. Eyes strained to the shore, a white handkerchief was pulled out and semaphored at arm's length, and sometimes I saw the tiny white returning flicker at the window or door of a high-perched house.

"How long," I asked a neighbor on the upper deck, "how long do you think these people have been away?"

"A week maybe," he said, and shrugged and smiled. "We are family people."

Yes, family people; that I was to see—family people and children-relishing people, islanders with a turning inward to community and family. We came to Calheta, pink and white and blue and pale-green, an enchanting huddle under the towering pile of crag, a little operetta town standing about the open space of quay, and there went ashore a young soldier. He stood straight and was rather darkly handsome, this young man, carrying his shabby uniform with an air. On the quay his family waited for reunion, and who could have said of so many who was brother, who cousin? But in all the embracing, the arm-entwining, there began to be a pattern; the girl, seventeen, eighteen perhaps—was she girl friend or young sister? Sister, I thought, adoring young sister, a little shy and standing close and gazing silently. The old woman in peasant black, crying a little, touching his arm and leaving her lingering hand, she must be mother. Of the swarm of small boys, those about whose thin shoulders the strong arm was laid were probably brothers, and those were cousins for whom there was a clasp of the hand. The reunion there on the quay was long, quietly tender, but with a sort of dignity, almost a sort of intimate ceremony.

And then Calheta was gone, faded into the insubstance of the long day. "Look," said my neighbor, "Pico." He touched my arm, pointed to the port bow, and there in the haze was a deeper haze that soon took form, became a smoky substance of land.

"First we go to Velas here on São Jorge, then we go across to Pico. Soon we shall see Fayal." He said "Fayal" as he might say "Paradise." "Fayal is my home."

So there was Pico, at last, an enigmatic shape of haze, Pico of which I knew. I knew it as a whaling island sharing pre-eminence with Fayal; I knew that just beyond lay Fayal. We continued under the towering hang of São Jorge, and Pico grew and filled the drift of distance. Now my neighbor took my arm again; he pointed, and I could see a vaguer shape beyond the ultimate smudge of Pico.

"Fayal," he said.

But now we were coming to Vila das Velas; I could see the tiny cluster of its color under the jagged heights, and soon, as we came into the quay, I saw that there was to be a festa. The boats lying at their moorings were being dressed overall with paper flags, red and blue, yellow and green and pink. And there, among them, surely legend made substance, was a whaleboat. There it was, dressed with flags as the others were, so frail a boat for its gargantuan purpose, so small in that context, but so elegant, as beautiful and clean of line as a boat could ever be. The hull was white, the strake below the gunwale green, the inside pink—a boat for so grim a task, but inevitably with that innate gaiety of decoration that is Portuguese. She lay there still and lightly as a toy on the deep green of the harbor water, and who, not knowing, could have guessed her purpose but for the harpoons and lances stowed in her bows? And now I saw that beyond her lay a whalers' motor towboat, low and rakish and sparely functional, though gay now with its dressing of flags. Here, then, was affirmation that the legend was no legend but reality; but how was I to have expected that the evidence should be so delighting? And what sort of people were these, of such ingenuous gaiety and warmth, so simply tranquil, but with such strange intrepidity?

Now *Espirito Santo's* siren sounded its outrageous blast, we were cast off, and São Jorge dropped astern; now we were going to Pico, and beyond Pico, Fayal was forming into substance. Upon the whole wild legend there was coming credibility; the mist that Pico had been was becoming solid, an upsoaring sweep into its crown of cloud, crenelated over its flanks with its family of minor volcanic cones. The little ship rode on, breasting over the swell, and then low and small and distant against the surf I could see Cais do Pico; and Cais do Pico I knew had a whaling station.

Then as we came in, I saw it, over to starboard; there was the slip, the flensing platform, and on it in front of the whale factory, figures moving about some business.

"They have just finished," my neighbor told me. "They have been cutting in a whale—they are cooking the blubber. Shall we walk over to see?"

But first we must go in to the quay and tie up; there was a difficulty, with shouting aboard and on the quay. A crewman ran to the stern with the long boathook, reaching over, fending off something. Then I saw a dinghy, grappled to a flocculent mass, towing it to clear it from fouling the ship's screw. All about us were such bloated islands of matter.

My friend was laconic. "Whales' guts," he said. "They tow them out to sea later."

Now we went in slowly, nosing through, and when we were tied up we went ashore, up the boat slip and along the white wall under the oleanders and acacia and oranges and turned the corner by the big dark olive tree. And then there was the whale factory, and what could a first impression of that be but its smell—pervasive, penetrating, fatty, oily, bringing an instant nauseous stirring? And those, at last, were whalemen; they trod the stones wide-legged with big spread feet and thick ankles still blooded, with loose linen pantaloons, white, blue-striped, patched and patched on patches, rolled to the calf. Conical straw hats with wide upturned brims shaded their broad brown faces and bold squinting seamen's eyes; they were leathery men, hide-tough and brown.

But now we heard *Espirito Santo's* ear-assaulting call; the last of the cargo—soap, white, blue-veined like Stilton cheese —was going aboard. Then we had cast off, Cais do Pico melted astern, and the journey was nearly done. We were coming to Fayal, forming now from haze to tangibility. Now I could see the rumple of her peaky heights, then there was the thread of her surf under the drop of precipice. We turned the tail of Pico's point, and the far pale mosaic of the little town against the shore was there. There was Horta, Horta on Fayal, Horta, which, as I knew, was almost the capital of Azorean whaling.

We turned past the long outflung arm of the mole, under the light; we were in Horta's harbor. In the low lambency of evening she had still, though now so close, the look of only half reality. She was delicately, lightly beautiful. More perfect a sight you could scarcely expect on common earth. Her frontages were painted, in the Portuguese fashion, with pastry cooks' colors—white and warm pink and eau de Nil and cerulean blue and dull rose—and this pale lilt of her color had the dark sharp accents of palms tall above the roofs.

Espirito Santo sidled to the quay, shuffled her car-tire fenders against the porous face of the volcanic stone, and then we were ashore. I had come to Horta.

I W E N T S T R A I G H T to João do Talho from the harbor, but not till next morning to Café Sport; but no matter which comes first, it is thus that intimacy with Horta and Fayal must begin. Through the filter of those two places, João's restaurant and Henrique's and José's little café, all of consequence in Fayal must sometime seep. And I, newly arrived, was taken (as new arrivals are) up from the harbor and through the cool cleft of the streets under the pale-painted façades, through the square with the tall dark palms and the Café International, through the other two squares with cool canopy of trees and blaze of bougainvillaea, and there was the little turn up to João's. It was a narrow way between white walls, unpaved and rough to the feet; João's swinging doors, pink and blue, opened above four stone steps.

It was square inside, high-ceilinged, with a naïve, would-be contemporary decor, so that the eye, denied a focus, wandered over walls and ceiling impartially patterned in pink and blue and buff. A corner partitioned off was the kitchen, and by its doorless entrance was the small wash basin with brass tap above so that, before eating, you might wash your hands. Around the walls the tables were ranged, and in the open central space stood João. We regarded each other, he and I as we were introduced, and his dark eyes had the long blinkless stare of one not concerned with the impression he makes. He was short, and rather stout, giving the impression a little of having been pressed from above, with flat-topped head and short neck set down in his open shirt between his braces. He said nothing, but stood and looked, and

his look was one of unhurried appraisal. Then the faint shadow of a smile came and was gone from the stillness of his face. He pointed to a table, and there, when I had sat, gave me the menu; I was to know it well.

Still the unanimated weight of his eyes was on me, and as I groped in blind incomprehension through the menu, trying with gesture and poverty of Portuguese to draw help from him, he said not a word. When I had plunged, ordered at a guess, he walked to the corner kitchen still silent, each shoe squeaking. The meal was large, strongly rich with oil and garlic; but his sidelong black-eyed gaze under arched brows was on me as he squeaked between tables and kitchen, and though satiation came quite soon, I felt a compulsion to push on against the wilt of appetite. I felt—and this was probably no fancy—that I was on probation; new as I was in Horta, I had heard of João.

He had his fame, a quirk of reputation. "The rudest man in Horta João is," and Norberto, who had told me, had laughed affectionately as he said it. There had been a man, gastrically troubled, who had come to João's.

"Now I have to be careful," he had said. "You mustn't give me anything rich. You can cook me a little steamed fish perhaps."

João had looked at him (I could guess his look), then he had pointed through the window, up the hill where the hospital lay.

"That's where you should eat," he said. "I serve food here."

With time, after that first night, I came to know João well; when at last the mask relaxed, and his smile came, it had a surprising sweetness; even, on a precious occasion, he put a friendly hand momentarily on my shoulder. To achieve so much demonstration from João had the warming sense of an accolade. Now, though, this first night, he was in his initial caution, his scrutiny; I ate, drank Pico wine, then left, all without winning a word.

In the morning the tranquil air was saturated with sun,

and as I walked past the Café International, through the pools of shade under the dark-crowned trees in the small square, the canaries were ecstatic among the leaves. Across the harbor and across the straits there was the sublimity of Pico's soaring peak, cloudless now, so perfect as to be hardly believed. It is high (over 7,000 feet), the highest mountain in the Azores; but it is not its height that so enchants—Fujiyama and Popocatepetl have no more idealized shape. On that southeastern side of Fayal there is no prospect not dominated by the peak of Pico when weather allows it. Again I had the sense (the sense that pervades discovery of the Azores) of the simmering volcanic undertone, the barely quiescent tremor beneath the peace. So for centuries the peak has stood, sublime and quiet, but even now its crown is warm; there, unexpected at that altitude, there are warmth-loving species of butterflies.

As I walked beyond the harbor, the town clustered on the neck of an isthmus that gives backing to the harbor; the streets, cramped within the slopes, tilted, wove into a small gay labyrinth that stacked up tiers of terraces on the hill above the harbor. Then, looking at the hill, I saw that it was no hill of earth and stone but a heap, a pile of volcanic ash and cinder, reddish and black, like a slag-heap hardly cool. Its name, as I was to learn, translated means "Burnt Mountain."

I came out from the brief tangle of the isthmus and there was a small bay, gentle-surfaced under the shelter of Burnt Mountain and that other higher hill, 1,000 feet perhaps, that was the end of the isthmus. And there, under the swell of the high hill, was a building, white, high-chimneyed. I leapt to recognition of it. This was the bay of Porto Pim; that was the whale factory. I could see, across the bay, the tunneled slip from the water to the flensing platform. So much I saw then;

there was so much I was to see and to learn later of Porto Pim.

Now I walked on; this was the outskirts of Horta, a straggle of houses above the sea, not high, flat-fronted like those of the streets, but low, spanned out with trellis and pergola and scramble of vine, throwing a dapple of shade on the pink walls. The men, because it was Sunday, lolled in the shade, staring with the curiosity of those who see few strangers; behind them, within the doors, there were the women and girls, as curious but affecting not to look. They, the men and the women, looked drowsily, with half-closed eyes because there was such an opulence of sun. Heavy swags of blossom, bougainvillaea and ipomoea, camellia and hibiscus, sagged from the white walls above the road. It was then, nearly out of the town, that I met Henrique.

He was aquiline and elderly, with a spare gray mustache. "Good morning," he said, and raised his broad-brimmed Homburg. "Come to my shop. My son speaks good English," and together we walked back into the town, going at his old-man's pace till we came to the harbor and up the rise of patterned pavement under the trees.

Then he stopped. "This is my shop." He bowed slightly, motioning me to the deep doorway in the narrow frontage of dull-blue painted wall. "Café Sport," said the faded red sign over the door. Just so, almost inconsequentially, I came first to Café Sport—or so at least it seemed. Its inevitability was not apparent then.

The café was small, with tables around the wall and a counter at the back. Behind the counter was José. His face was one that twinkled with friendliness; his light-brown eyes were screwed a little from much smiling.

"Good morning," he said from behind the jars of candy and crackers, "Welcome to Horta and Café Sport."

He could as well have said, "Welcome to Café Sport"; welcome there bestows the key to Horta, though I had still to learn that.

"I am José Azevedo and that is my father, Henrique Azevedo—but I am always called Peter. What do you think of Horta—and why do you come here from so far away in England?"

I spoke of the enchantment that Horta had for me, and

then told him that it was for the whaling that I had come, that perhaps I would write a book about it. Peter smiled his twinkling smile, showing his pleasure in my pleasure in Horta, and from that moment he made the contributing of help to my exploration his responsibility. He became my friend, his café my center; from its intimacy ended or started all my goings.

You would hardly notice Café Sport if you had no cognizance of it; it has a retired and unpretentious air. It lies in that mall-like street, tree-shaded, where the town begins to rise away from the harbor, lifting away to its levels above the sea. Opposite the café's door, across the street, is a low wall where you may sit on sunny mornings to watch the boats and the high-flung arms of the fishermen in the quickly rising and quickly dying tempests of their arguments. And, sitting with your drink at Café Sport's little tables, you may see in the frame of its door the harbor with the broad shine of the five-mile straits beyond, and beyond that the soaring serenity of the peak of Pico.

It commands the harbor, that doorway; no event, no arrival, no departure can escape its aerie watch. To know the maritime pulse of Horta, to know the movement of the merest dinghy or of all the stately ocean-crossing yachts that call, you have only to while away the easy hours there. Lieutenant Commander Rui Mourão de Castro, Captain of the Port, in his office by the harbor, has the intimacy of knowledge that his command gives; but Peter, behind his candy jars, probably has as concise a view. And, indeed, his binoculars are always within reach.

Skippers old to the game, knowing their Azores, come as inevitably through the little door of Café Sport as they put foot upon the quay; first-timers do not know the certainty of their being drawn into Peter's kindly web—nor do they know, perhaps never do know, that before their anchor's dropped, the complement aboard is known in Café Sport. But, old or new, by intention or not, for most mariners the way across the North Atlantic lies through the Café Sport. Fifty-five days a Brazilian yacht had come to pass with magnetic certainty through that needle's eye; and so had come the lofty American yacht, with its curving tumble-home, and a tiny tub, twenty feet, no more, sailed by two English boys. The pull of the place, the gravitational certainty of it, let it be admitted, is Peter's business; not only does he preside above the candy jars, serve his drinks, he is also a ships' chandler.

But Peter is no counter of cold coin, no mere man in business; he has a vocation. Through his doorway in the blue wall he feels the span and air of all the ocean; he, as it were, *collects* its traffic. His pleasure is in its needs. You may want one brass bolt for a tackle or a hundred fathoms of manila; Peter will fix it—and if, as is common, he gets the price reduced, that is his satisfaction.

The life of Fayal itself has as close a focus through the little café as that of the ocean, and you may meet almost the highest and the humblest over its tables. The taste and texture of Fayal, the sense of its present and its past, its humid air, its opulent soil, its time-ignoring leisureliness, all that, all the spirit of Fayal is to be felt in Café Sport; and inescapably, the sense of its whaling. It was there, in Café Sport, that I learned that the queer emotional threads of whaling are woven through the entire being of Fayal—that, indeed, whaling *is* a sort of ultimate expression of it, of the odd amalgam that is Fayalese. The men I met there, swart sloe-eyed men, blue-eyed men, lean tough men and short rotund men, were all Fayal men, only partly Portuguese, and more specially the island's indigenous race. They had a kind of par-

ticular crucibled separateness; their past and their environ-
ment seemed to have produced a concurrence of leisured
serenity and half-slumbering combustiveness. Only some of
Fayal's men are whalers; the sense of whaling, however, the
hot fidget of it is in all.

Nowadays we would call it an ambivalence, a love-hate;
the tragedy and the exultation, the danger and the belly-
thrumming thrill, are dual concomitants. These men of Fayal
will ignite with talk of whaling, become terse and low and
thrilled, then almost in a breath tell you with melancholy
of the grisly tragedies of the hunt.

One placid desultory evening in Café Sport there was at
my table Manuel Botelho, who is a fisherman; we and others
were drinking Pico wine, and conversation turned, as it will,
to whaling.

"When I was a little boy I was one of five brothers—
Manuel, which was I, Francisco, Antonio, Camil, Eduardo—
and our father was a whaler. Oh, and how I remember it. My
father he go to sea because there was a whale, and he harpoon the whale. But then they had to tow the whale to
shore rowing the *canoa*,[1] and for two days and three nights
they row. And the first night I say, 'Mama, why Papa no
come?' And then there was all next day and next night and
another day and night after that, and all the time I say,
'Mama, why Papa no come?' and Mama she cry because she
think Papa never come no more. Then on the third day I
see Papa's *canoa* coming, towing the whale, and I shout,
'Mama, Papa he come. Mama, Papa he come.' Then Mama
she cry because Papa come."

For all that, Manuel said, his father was paid three
escudos (three "*shcoots*" is the way of saying it), and that,

[1] Canoa *is the Azorean name for the whaleboat, and how that
came to be shall be explained later.*

in 1915, was about $1.80, and bread at that time cost four-and-a-half centavos, say 4¢. Then as now, the rate of payment for whaling was the slightest of inducements—the payment docs no more than make possible what a man of Fayal feels so much compulsion to do. Seamen of Portugal have never been other than intrepid; they have always been hardy and courageous. But in these men of the Azores there is some other smoldering core, some itch to extremities of hazard. I became curious and then, I think, perceptive; I learned by degrees enough of the islands' history and physical nature to think that in that lay an explanation—an explanation of why Manuel, having told me of that childhood's nightmare, went on with verve to talk of his own whaling days.

Positive history for the Azores begins about the year 1432, when they were discovered by the ships of Prince Henry the Navigator, though "discovery" is only relative in this context. In the fourteenth century the maps of Catalan and Genoese seamen showed the Azores—Fayal was called Isla de Ventura—and there is even a shadow of possibility that the islands were known to the Arabs and Phoenicians. But with the coming of the Portuguese the earlier name was superseded; it became Fayal, though not without some competitive interchange. Prince Henry called it São Luiz in honor of St. Louis of France, and, for a while, it was Nova Flandria because there were so many Flemish colonists. Finally, and perhaps the better so, it was Fayal.

It is in the Flemish colonization that, I believe, there is to be isolated one of the parts of the formula that has made the Azorean man. The first systematic colonization was in 1466, and it was a Flemish one in the care of Josse (or Jos) de Hurtere; he was a Flemish nobleman, appointed Lord Lieutenant of Fayal. More Flemings came until, in 1490, it was estimated that there were 1,500 in Fayal. But, concurrently, Portuguese had been coming in large groups and, at least politically and culturally, assimilated the Flemings; so the record says, but "assimilated," so used, may not be truly descriptive. Visual evidence of that far-off mixing is abundant today, and all experience shows that the crossing of two very dissimilar strains does not produce the submerging of the lesser in the more dominant, but something different, not one or the other, something, often, with a peculiar potency not belonging to either.

The windmills that are everywhere to be found in the Azores, still working, are concrete and unchanged reminders of the Flemish heritage, but Horta's name may be more symbolic. Its perpetuation of the name of Jos de Hurtere acknowledges its Flemish origin but has taken on an outwardly Portuguese form—and that indeed is like the people, something which is Azorean and nothing else. That same name, Hurtere, incidentally, remains commemorated in another way; descendants with a corrupted form, Dufra, still live in Fayal.

And so with Fayal's men, those men I knew so well, about the harbor, in Café Sport. Some had an indubitable Portuguese darkness, swarthy men whose eyes were black lakes under their heavy lashes; but some were fair men, light-haired, with eyes not merely blue but with a sharp gem-like glitter of blueness. And those you might have said, if you saw them in repose, were an unmodified continuance of the old Flemish stock; but for that you must see them for only the shortest time. They, like any Azorean, were quick of mood, quick as their dark kinsmen to alternate from gentleness to explosive argument, from placidity to hot gesticulation. In them and in the dark ones there was to be felt the smolder within the sweetness.

But this ethnology reflects as much, I think, the physical nature of the Azores—and here it is to be noted that though the Azores as one entity have so strong and probably unique a character, each of the islands is none but itself; each is intensely individual. Each too has an intensity of another kind, a sense of eruptiveness, almost as if the mutter of it might be caught. Fayal is a peaceful place; its tranquillity, its sense of removal from all further worlds is almost tangible. It has almost a texture. But very soon comes the consciousness of a surge, a thrust, beneath the peace. First there is the awareness of the astonishing scope of its flora, of how multitudinous the range of plants and trees is; exotics and temperates rampage from the ashy crumble of the volcanic soil. A clothespin, you are prepared to believe, would burgeon and blossom if planted there.

The growth which sprawls and scrambles, trails and clambers from the sea's edge to the island's cratered crown is an inextricable mingling of what is indigenous, what has been introduced, and what has escaped from the order of the gardens. In other places there will be escapes from gardens, quite timid venturers from security; but here it cannot be imagined that a garden could contain its inmates. They burst out, make a riot. Climbing white roses have come out of the gardens, taken to the hills, and for the whole eye's reach either way have made of themselves a dense and fragrant hedge. *Hydrangea hortensia,* so trim and domestic a shrub in the gardens of England and America, in Fayal is dense by every road, sprawling down the lava gullies, climbing almost to the island's summit. There is the feeling indeed that such perfervid growth is an expression of a simmer in the soil, an exuberance coming from an inner heat—and that, of course, it is.

This island, like all the archipelago, is volcano-built; long-gone furies of boiling rock threw it up. And, though those events are so far down the slope of time, though the cooling eons have given soil and peace and settlement, the heat is in the heart of it still. Sometimes the hot breath of that interior bursts out; to Fayal on September 27, 1957, there came such a thing. On that day, after four days of minor earth tremors, a fuming discolored bubbling broke upon the sea half a mile off the coast of Capelinhos, and from then until October 25, 1958, there was continual violent eruption. Such a fury of steam, smoke, and ash towered from the sea within the first days—a column 3,000 feet high—that in less than a month it had built an island 450 feet high. But this, on October 25, disappeared in just twenty-four hours, and, as it seemed, made a prelude for the violence to follow. It came some days later with a huge laboring of roars, bangs, lightning, with a hurling out of ash and rock that soon had formed a new island and joined it to the Capelinhos coast. The lava flow began on December 17, and, while the enormity of explosions continued, the volcano cloud rose to 25,000 feet. It was visible from Terceira. So, throughout winter and spring, eruption went on; earth tremor was nearly continuous, the earth roared and rumbled and threw out a sulfurous vomit of ash and clinker. From the crater and other vents the lava flowed.

The night of May 12–13 was one that now, so long after, is told of with a lowering of the voice. "We did not know how that night would end," they say, and tell you of the 450 earthquakes that rumbled through the quivering foundations of the whole island. In the area of Praia do Norte such was the ferocity that 500 houses were destroyed, and I have seen them, tumbled stone ghosts half hidden now in rampant growth. All the eruption till this night had been in the Capelinhos place of origin, but in this night there came a

fissure right over the high crest of the island, and there, at
the island's center, in the Caldeiro, the great crater, a gas-
emitting vent appeared as a great bang burst out of the
earth. Coincidentally the lava flow at Capelinhos increased
and soon had built a cone 500 feet high. At last, on October
25, the eruption ended, leaving a hang of smoke and steam
over the crest of the new cone and an extension of the island
of over a square mile.

Time, a healing passage of years, has passed since then,
and now you may go to Capelinhos and see the relict desert
there and think that thus, no doubt, the whole island was in
its undiscovered youth. Now, after the sulfurous din, there
is silence. You go by the narrow road that twists and clings
around the high flanks of the island; you pass the shattered
crumble of Praia do Norte, then abruptly the road stops. It is
lost in a deep blanket of red and ashy dust; there are no more
houses, no more growth, in the distance just the remnant of
the lighthouse, tumbled, half-buried, on what was the island's edge. A steep decline falls away, and at first as you go,
slipping, stumbling through the litter of cooled clinker-like
gray stone sponges, there is a remnant of growth, charred
spikes of shrubs standing dead from the ash and, still, a
pattern of the little cultivated areas shown by emergent
spikes of that giant grass, *Arundo donax*, that is used in the
Azores to hedge the plots.

Then that ends, all ends; there is utter desolation. You
come to the bottom of the decline and climb slowly toward
the lighthouse's ghostly remnant, laboring in the deep sink
of ash, eyes filled and ears filled, enclosed by the silence and
negation. By the lighthouse at last you are on the brink, on
the edge that was the land's last plunge to the sea, but which
now hangs over the deep dead valley that lies between the
lighthouse and the stark red lifeless cone of the volcano. In
the bottom you can see the lava flow, cold and stopped now,

as still and dead and immobilized as all else. Then you see the sea birds, circling and sweeping through the crater's rim, and you hear faintly in the silence their cries. That one germ of life reminds you that time will restore life here, build soil, and then it will have the bursting ebullience of life that Fayal's soil has, that volcanic soil has.

Then you have the long slipping scrambling walk back with shortening breath until there is the car again and you take off your shoes to empty out the ash and gaze luxuriously at the green riot of growth. Perhaps because of the luxury of it after the silent desert behind, you are attentive, more observing. You see the small abundance of the garden plots by the houses; you see the extravagance of the little orchards, if those rich tangles may be called such—apples and loquats, plums and oranges, pears and peaches, and the scrambling abandon of the vines—no inch of cultivable space not bearing exuberantly. Then you look beyond, at the downsweeps from the soaring heights, all the volcanic cones that are minor to the great central one, and see that they are green to their tops in scrub growth. The dropping slopes are lava slides and gullies, compacted ash screes, and by some miracle of fertility there is rooting there.

In these places, these shrub forests, you will always find faya, a little dark tree, tall shrub if you like, slim-stemmed, with richly dark green leaves pale-backed. It is indigenous and ubiquitous and, it may be guessed, its prevalence impressed the early settlers; they gave its name to the island. And, as often, you will see that giant heather, *Erica azorica*, six and seven feet high, which is as peculiarly Azorean, and the oleanders, pink and white. Natives they are, but about the houses along the road clinging under the heights there are strange exotics—there is the dragon tree with its stout pallid bole and bare twist of limbs and cactus-like crown of broad sword-leaves.

From this narrow road that makes a circlet of the island, another debouches and climbs twisting and doubling through a shade of eucalyptus and faya and high-banked hydrangea to reach the Caldeiro, the great crater that is parent to all those others that pock the tops of every height. There the road ends, on the roof of the island, by the crater, and it has a final perfection of what a crater may be just as the peak of Pico is a finality of what perfection a volcanic peak may have.

The crater is four miles in circumference and 1,300 feet deep, but what do figures convey of the silent wind-clean awesomeness of that vast bowl, its silence, the shadowed stillness of its depth, its utter final loneliness, the perfect symmetry of its plunge from the clean cut of its periphery? What can you think of in the haunting of its silence but the unimaginable enormity of its making? You watch the buzzard wheeling far below within the plunge and remember that in the Capelinhos eruption so short a time ago, that remote floor of the pit opened again, belched its sulfur again. There, in the ultimate peace, the sense is strong of the sulky hot heart of the island. You turn from the crater and see drawn across the nearby summit the long line of the fissure that came on the night of May 12–13, 1958.

Then you drop down the road, drop back to the reassurance of the humanized levels of the island, and when, soon, you go into the café by the road, there are the men you know, warm simple Fayalese, friendly gentle-mannered men, and you drink Verdelho with them, that robust fine white wine from Pico. But the sense of the crater is with you still, the sense of the quiet deep smolder in the island's heart under the flowering peace, and again you think that your perception of these men of Fayal is growing. You can understand that whaling should be, as you see it to be, obsessional with such men.

TH E   SP E A K I N G of English on Fayal is not uncom-
mon; the English spoken, though, is of two kinds. Younger
generations, all but the elderly indeed, have an English which,
however strong its Portuguese inflection, derives in accent
from England. It is so the children learn it in school, so most
people up to middle age speak it. The elderly are otherwise;
theirs is the English of New England—of New Bedford, of
Nantucket. They are survivors of the old days, those times
when Horta's harbor was crowded with New England whaleships. They are gone now, long gone; in 1921 the last whaleship called at Horta. The whaleships come no more, but
theirs is the legacy that gave Fayal and all the Azores its
sperm-whaling industry, which, the stuff of history, of old
stories as it is in New England, lives on in the Azores in its
strange isolated entirety. The sperm whale is still hunted
elsewhere, hunted with awful efficiency beyond its continuing capacity for survival. Just in the Azores (and a little in
Madeira) the old way goes on.

In this there is another part, if not of blood, of the peculiar separateness of the Azores—of their being, though Portuguese, still more and particularly Azorean. Their association with New England in the nineteenth century was a profound one, and that has tinctured all of life, become a part now of the indigenous whole—or so anyway it is in Fayal, and I may speak positively only of what I have seen.

From the start the New Englanders, coming in their whaleships, found in the Azoreans an instant response to the rough wild hazard that whaling was. It may even be guessed that it was for just such a thing that the incandescence of the Azorean character had been waiting. Conjecture though that is, the evidence supports it well; in 1765, the whaleships out of Nantucket came first to Fayal. They had scoured their nearer seas and, pressing farther, came to the waters of what then they called the "Western Islands grounds," the deep Atlantic waters of the Azores. It may be imagined that it appeared to them a whaling Eldorado, because they found not only so rich an abundance of sperm whales, but also these islanders for whom the searing dangers of whaling were a sort of inspiration. It does appear indeed that the Azoreans had before then, at some earlier time, caught whales and caught them from the shore. Robert Clarke, as eminent an authority on Azorean whaling as may be found, suggests that the early Basque whalers are likely to have come to the Azores, and he points to the use today in the islands of the word *vigias* for the lookouts who from their precipice vantages scan the sea for whales. *Vigias* is a Basque word, and so is *cachalote*; in Fayal you will nearly as often hear the sperm whale called *cachalote* as you will hear it called *baleia*, the Portuguese word for whale.

But whatever the effect of earlier experience, Azorean adaptation to whaling was immediate and secure; the methods, the skills, they acquired quickly, but as I know, they must have brought to it too their peculiarly apt temperament. Robert Clarke quotes a source about 1855.

> A great many Western Island Portuguese find employment in American whalemen [that is, whaling ships], almost every vessel sailing from New Bedford carrying more or less of them. They are quiet, peaceful, inoffensive people, sober and industrious, penurious almost to a fault, and I believe invariably excellent whalemen.[1]

That, as far as it goes, is true, but it is a partial truth because it is superficial. It has no perception of the further Azorean qualities. Those virtues so approvingly declared the Azorean undoubtedly has (in his own way), but it leaves out his inner gusto, his volcanic verve. And the unqualified statement of those so-solid virtues amounts to inaccuracy—inaccuracy which is relevant to his ideal aptitude for open-boat whaling. "Inoffensive"? Yes, so he is if his easy unselfconscious courtesy and kindliness may be called so. "Peaceful"? That too, but he will erupt instantly and subside as soon for a point of argument or friction. And "sober"; yes that he may be called also, but in his own special fashion, Azoreans (as I have seen them) have a gay unaffected enjoyment of drink; they enjoy it lightly, happily, like enjoying sun. They grow up to the enjoyment of it from childhood as they do to any other part of the happiness of life; but I would call them sober.

There was a day when I was at sea with the whalers, in the stern with the skipper and the stroke oar; the hunt had flagged because the sighted whale had sounded and been

---

[1] *Robert Clarke, "Open Boat Whaling in the Azores,"* Discovery Reports, Vol. 26 (*Cambridge, England: Cambridge University Press;* 1954) *pp. 281–354.*

lost, and now in the desultory pause which had come we lay in the sea's wallow and turned to our food. The whalers, as is their way, had their bread and their water in the big wine jars; but I had wine, and offered it to those two with me in the stern. They declined it with the infinite and endearing grace of courtesy of their kind, Manuel, who was skipper, telling me, yes, ashore he would like wine, but not at sea. In the finality of that refusal there was a sudden glimpse of the delicate certainty of judgment that the crises of whaling demand. It is so, in such a context, that these are sober men, as they would be anything that the dangers of their craft demand. They are brave men, inspiredly intrepid men, but never foolhardy, never careless with dangers that may threaten not only their own lives but the lives too of those with whom they sail.

It is apparent that the New England whaleship skippers found the Azorean men providentially apt for whaling, and through the nineteenth century the Azoreans became increasingly predominant in the crews of the ships—and, latterly, after 1900 to the end of the New England whaleship era about 1920, it was mainly on the quarter-deck they were to be found, as mates or masters.

And now, when all that is passed, when the New England ships come no more and no whalers go upon the seas from New Bedford and Nantucket and only the Azores still live that old history, there is still there in the islands the old vocabulary, the old salty jargon. The men of Fayal and Pico and the rest who now go in open boats to hunt the sperm whale are more often younger men than older; they are men, mainly, who never knew the whaleship days, who never saw or heard New Englanders. But, still, the words they use, the technical words of whaling, are New England words rendered phonetically into Portuguese. "There she blows!" the New Englanders said, and *bloz!* the Azoreans say, and the sound of it is virtually the same. The New Englanders said "cleat"; the Azoreans say *clît*, and that too is the same in sound; and so, almost, is *blequesquine* for "blackskin" and *bûme* for "boom." And *logaête*, however different it looks, is very like "loggerhead" when spoken. "Hump" is *ampo*, "case" is *queize*, and so it is with all the whaling words, and it is curious that the genuinely Portuguese equivalents for many of these words are not used or even known by the Azorean whalers.

The most interesting of these transpositions from New England is the word for the whaleboat itself, and no other word will you ever hear used in the Azores; the word is *canoa*. Its heredity is as aromatic as old ship's rope. The whalemen of the whaleships hunted from lowered boats, and the need was for craft that, above all, should be maneuverable and lively of handling rather than sturdily seaworthy. The need, as always, evolved its answer, and by the logic of the need the boats were like the Indian canoes which had been evolved from similar needs. The whaleboats were bigger, stronger because they were sea boats, but their descent was acknowledged; the whalers called them canoes. Azorean whaleboats are bigger than those old lowered boats (and the reason will be explained), but otherwise they are the same, the same in the light elegance that comes of their functional needs. *Canoa* the word is spelled, but its pronunciation is *canooa*.

There are still men in Horta, old men, who remember the latter years of the New England era; Senhor Lucas da Silva recalls the harbor forested with whaleship masts, and he, as a boy, knew the whalemen well.

"Often there would be ten or fifteen whaleships in the harbor—it was in the autumn of the year they came and they would have crewed the ships in the Cape Verde Islands and, sometimes, in the West Indies too. Mostly they would stay for five weeks, and would discharge their cargo of oil; sometimes a ship would discharge as much as a thousand barrels of oil, sometimes more.

"I remember too that toward the end of their time here some of the American crew would desert and lose themselves back in the hills among the farmers there. Then boys of Fayal here would take the chance—wishing to avoid military service, you see—to smuggle themselves aboard as crewmen. Sometimes a whole Yankee crew, cook, deck-hands, everyone, would desert, and the ship would be in difficulty as to how to sail. These American crewmen would go and get free board and lodging from the farmers back there in the hills, and would give clothing in exchange. The farmers were glad to help anyway—most of them you see had relatives in the United States. 'Because of our relatives,' they would say, 'the least we can do is help these poor devils.'

"Often the police would come searching for the American deserters because, of course, the ships were desperate. But the farmers—they used to grind their corn in those many windmills back there—had a system for warning the deserters. They had horns, you see, that they used with the cattle. 'When you hear these horns,' they said, 'hide away; it means the police are coming.'

"And the Azorean boys used to hide up around the harbor, waiting for a chance to slip aboard—and the customs officers knew this and used to be aboard to prevent them; but often they were not successful. But, still, that did make it difficult for the boys to get aboard, and there used to be all sorts of tricks, good ones sometimes too, and so the customs cutter would follow the whaleship to sea to take off the Azoreans —but there would be tricks for that too.

"There was a ship that was sailing at night, and it put a light on a barrel and set it adrift so that the cutter would go off pursuing *that*. Then the ship slipped quietly from its anchorage and went to an agreed point where it picked up the Azoreans waiting there."

Senhor Lucas da Silva speaks easy fluent English, New England English, and his learning of it was probably typical of many of his generation in Horta. His father kept a boarding house, and, often, the customs men would capture a party of American deserters and bring them there to await extradition. It was common for the house to be full of New England whalemen, and he, a small boy, was constantly with them, talking to them, playing games with them, asking what is this, what is that. His easy command of English, Nantucket English, is a sort of memorial to those old times that were parent to Azorean whaling. Sometimes, he said, the American crewmen would get drunk—but they were no real trouble, never anything that could not be coped with.

So close did the association of Azoreans and the whaleships of New England become during the nineteenth century, so identified indeed did whaling everywhere become with Azoreans, that it was inevitable that there should have been a Portuguese venture. The government, in continental Portugal, had long wanted a national whaling industry, but the continental Portuguese—and this stresses again the separateness of the Azoreans—had little taste for the raw rough labors and dangers of the trade. Who can blame them for that? But the Azoreans had become skilled and experienced whalemen, and on the basis of that, Portuguese whaleships were fitted out and, for a period, worked the seas of Portugal and her overseas territories—Brazil, the Cape Verde Islands, Mozambique. Even the Azores fitted out ships, and soon after the mid-nineteenth century there were five, perhaps more, whaleships out of Horta. It was a venture of short life; it soon declined, and was certainly extinct by the end of the century.

There were economic reasons; shipowners were dubious of the risks of whaling, and this was coincident with the coming of shore whaling, which, it may have been felt, was more suited to the special Azorean aptitude, however successful Azoreans had been as whaleship crewmen.

Quite early, long before the end of the whaleship period, the better part of a century before, shore whaling in the Azores had its beginning. There is no documentary evidence for the date, but the verbal tradition among the whalers (and that is probably reliable) is insistent upon the year 1832, and it is equally positive that it was from Fayal that those pioneering boats were launched. How that first venture fared there is no history to tell, but its early abandonment suggests not well. There is evidence that the initiative for that start was an American one; it appears that it could have been a member of the American settler family named Dabney. When in the 1850s shore whaling began again, it was undoubtedly Dabney, with the Portuguese Bensaude, who was the initiator—and, this time, successfully. Shore whaling prospered and continued, and today you will see on, a building overlooking the harbor at Horta the name Bensaude and Co.

It was an American who was the pioneer, but it was the Azorean aptitude which he was deploying—it is the essence of this that whaling then, whaling of the old kind, was a thing of boats and boatmanship. Ships, the whaleships, were a means of conveying the boats and the boatmen to the place of the hunt, and, subsequently, of the treatment of the killed whale—the "cutting in" of the whale and the "trying out" of the blubber. The crucial part, the racking sequence between, was something of boats and of men of a kind able to live with such excruciating (and often malignant) adventure. None were so exactly molded in that kind as the islanders were.

Dabney saw that and he saw how providentially the nature of the islands paralleled that of the men. These are volcanic islands, and, characteristically, they fall to the sea almost everywhere by awesome sheers of precipice. From their lofty vantages, from lookouts so sited that their arcs of vision intersected, the whole surrounding ocean could be scanned. Where then was the need for ships? All the functions they had served could be served as well or better by the islands.

From the 1850s onward, then, shore whaling established itself and slowly spread and grew; and this growth was concurrent with much of the whaleships' heyday. It is apparent retrospectively that the whaleships' end about 1920 was inevitable, and that even then, for at least one decade before, they must have seemed an anachronism; but any contemporary observer, surely, would have held no higher hope for the future of shore whaling. As the shadow of hyperindustrialized whaling, of modern factory ships, of all the modern riskless methods began to fall, what could have looked a more ready victim than something as primitive, as nakedly dangerous, and piecemeal, as this? It would have been said, surely, that economics alone must end it—and so no doubt economics would have done but, again, for the peculiar singularity of the Azorean character. The economic structure of Azorean whaling is not one that allows or ever has allowed worthy rewards for the men; now, at least, if not always in the past, they have other occupations, often fishing—but these they leave the instant the rocket goes which signals the sighting of a whale. It may be said of latter-day whaling, if not of the past, that if the monetary reward were the only inducement, crews could not be found.

Only some of the men, lookouts, enginemen, skippers, and harpooners, are paid a retainer around the year, and that could not be called competitive, a mere $4.80 to $7.20 a month. Apart from that, crews are paid a monthly salary, a far from enticing one, and a variable percentage of the sale of products from the whale. Of that, 50 per cent of the selling price, a fully qualified whaler gets two shares and a semi-qualified whaler one share. Fully qualified men are those mentioned above. Crewmen, apart from skipper and harpooner, are semi-qualified men.

It cannot be said that even that scale of payment is *no* inducement, because the Azores are and have always been a poor community (though so happy a one); it can be said, I think, that the payment is enough to allow Azoreans to succumb to doing what they have such a temperamental demand to do.

The reservation above as to whether the monetary inducement had power enough in the past relates particularly to Pico, though probably it had significance too in the other islands. I have said that though the whole archipelago has so strong a corporate character, each island has its own intense individuality; Pico has at least as separate a character as any. Some of the islands have, as Fayal has, a fervent capacity for varied growth, but on Pico, only the lower skirts of its aspiring peak are habitable and growth there is little but the relatively worthless faya and the vines. Those vines were, till 1853, an asset robust enough to provide a major means of income for the island; wine was exported, and that known as Pico Madeira had a minor fame—it was probably that very palatable fortified white wine now called *verdelho*. But, in 1853 the vine louse phylloxera came; it devastated the vines, and the men of Pico must have been ready enough to find in the new shore whaling an alternative means of making their living.

Perhaps because for them it had a more desperate importance, perhaps because even among Azoreans Pico men are resiliently strong, they throve on shore whaling beyond the other islands; even, in time, winning concessions from the other islands for Pico boats and crews to be stationed on them. Their boats are to be seen today on Fayal, at Salão. And, still, Pico whalemen have the same separateness, the same overwhelming impression of leather-tough, salt-seasoned, spread-shouldered strength as their forefathers—whalemen of Fayal, bold, enduring, resolute as they are, do not give this immediate effect of thewy strength. Life on Pico, perhaps, has always conditioned men more hardily than on the other islands.

But on Pico or on Fayal—or any of the islands—life for most men was never other than for the enduring, and that is part reason for the continuance of open-boat whaling in spite of its enormous improbability. It must be assumed that, as the world goes now, so remote a relic cannot survive very long—perhaps a decade, perhaps two—though history since 1920 has already shown how rash prophecy can be. Who, then, in 1920, could have declared that forty-odd years hence would see the whalers of the Azores still in their so vulnerable confrontations with their awesome quarry? None but the whalers themselves perhaps. The interim has seen whaling elsewhere become so lethally mechanized, so freed from danger for those who pursue it, that one species at least, the blue whale, has been brought to the edge of extinction. Disrepute, culpably enough, has fallen on whaling at large, and perhaps the smear could touch the whalers of the Azores, little as they can be compared to the impersonally devastating butchery of modern factory ships.

It would be as apt to couple food-hunting with bow and

arrow with a modern abattoir. Azorean whaling belongs to
the old intrinsic place of man in the whole ecological frame,
a frame within which predation between the species was an
essential—and indeed still is; it is only the maladjustment
of a predatory ecology by man's modern devices that has
obscured that. However much pale factory-fed apartment
dwellers may shake horrified heads, man in his proper place
in nature *is* a predator. People, secure in towns, may be ad-
monitory about predation by men; they do not escape their
guilt (if such they consider it). They have delegated their
predation; they live by it while escaping the act. It is the
gross overgrowth of town populations, with their exploded
needs, that produces such plague-like distortions of predation
as modern whaling.

In the Azores now there is no sense that whaling as they
pursue it may not be perpetual. Its traceable history now is
only 137 years, but its nature is deep in the bone of Azorean
life; it has its lore, its tradition. Its festivals mark the year.
A tendency to *festas* is, truly enough, an important and
constantly recurrent part of Portuguese life—and how wist-
fully beautiful a part I have sometimes seen it to be—
but in the Azores *festas* have become (as everything must)
entwined with the thought and feeling of whaling. On Fayal
the whalers have their own *festa*, that of Nossa Senhora da
Guia which comes in August, but they have at least some
specialized involvement in all—they will not, during *festa*,
put to sea for whales, because that would induce calamity.
So it is during any *festa*, for they are all religious celebrations
and whalers are deeply Catholic men; so how much more
so during those *festas* which belong to saints of the whalers.
Whaling stations have their own saints; there is Senhora do
Socorro, who is saint of Salão and whose *festa* falls on the
second of September. But it is Senhora da Guia who is pre-
eminent in the whalers' year.

Festa dos baleieros her day is called, and when it comes, on the first Sunday in August, the whaleboats come from Fayal's two whaling stations, Salão and Varadouro, and are beached on the sharp dark volcanic sand of Porto Pim bay, under Burnt Mountain, against the whaling factory and the sea-jutting height of Monte da Guia. Crews and boats are dressed out in their best, the men in dark stiff suits and the boats overall with little flags. Then, processionally, up the narrow rough road that winds the flanks of Monte da Guia, go the crews to the tiny church dizzily poised above the sea —a church which is as well a lookout. There the dedication service is performed, the only service there in all the year —though, I have been told, marriages may sometimes be made in the little church.

When the service is over a procession forms to go slowly down the twist of road, treading over the flowers strewn underfoot, under the arches of green boughs set up by the men of the whale factory, preceded by a band and bearing the image of the Virgin and Child. With rockets and firecrackers they come again to Porto Pim bay where the boats wait, with line tubs uncovered and the line taken around the loggerhead and harpoons and a lance laid out in the bows. Now to each boat the priest comes, and at each the image of the saint is put athwart the boat, forward of the loggerhead, looking out to sea; the harpooner takes a double of whaleline around the saint, ties it loosely, and the boat is blessed. So, symbolically, the whalemen attach to themselves the being and protection of the saint; so, devoutly, they seek that they may catch whales and come safely from the hunt.

But it was earlier, in May, that I was first at a *festa*, that of Espirito Santo, one of the year's great festivals; for three days it transcends all else, no whaleman goes to sea, and a kind of unity of being comes upon the people. There are, for these suspended days, no rich, no poor, none but the people. In every home, in every place, no food is eaten but that of the ritual: the sweet bread—*massa cevada,* made of eggs and butter and flour—bread soup, veal, sweet rice. A serenity lies upon the place then, a sense of holiday, but quiet, a sort of bliss; on all and everyone is a smiling gentleness, and in the sweet courtesy of the time I was invited to the feast of Espirito Santo at Areeiro. It is the custom there, in this small village straggled on the heights above Varadouro, that each year one of its citizens shall be host to all the others on the Sunday of Espirito Santo, that he shall provide the food and the wine and with his own hands serve it to them. In the village hall the long tables ran from end to end tightly squeezed, all generations, whole families in best satins and dark pressed suits. Between the tables up and down with wine jug and dishes, gently quiet, smiling, was the host, a lean brown aging whaleman. His helpers, girls and young women, fluttered like butterflies, pausing, stooping, fluttering on, stooping again.

The soup came in huge vessels, great reservoirs placed at intervals along the tables, pale clear soup with its floating bread, and my neighbors were politely anxious, solicitous—was the soup good, did I like Espirito Santo soup? And so with the veal, and then the sweet rice, and I quailing with my own incapacity before the large generosity of it.

Outside, when it was done, there was a charmed interminability of conversation, groups drifting and changing and mixing, and the darkly handsome family with the beautiful little daughter allowing me for a while to hold their baby boy, as round and brown and softly smooth as an opening bud, with eyes like great round cushions of black velvet. The raveled tissue of timelessness was spun through all, and as the throng began to flake away I went with Herberto and others to the house of his grandparents, and they in their

timid courtesy were gently hospitable. The *massa cevada*
was put upon the table and the wines and fig brandy—
grown in the garden, made in the house—came out.

Twilight had passed and the soft dark come when we
left. Along the road the people still walked, this way and
that, still spellbound; when we came into the low light cast
by the oil pressure lamps of the café below the road, it was
crowded.

It was convivial there, shoulder to shoulder, and when I
had edged up to the counter there was Bert behind it, Bert
and his father; Bert was little and chirpy, as lively as a
sparrow.

"I went to Canada years ago—back now to fetch my
dad—he's old, see, on his own; not right for the old man.
They call me Bert over there."

Was that short for Humberto, I asked?

"Say—ain't that good! How'd you guess that?" Bert
beamed expansively and gave me a glass of Pico wine.

In the happy press against the counter, in the smoke and
talk and laughter and the hiss of the lamp above, I found
there was an old man beside me. He was weathered and
wrinkled; an old whaler, they said, too old now for that. His
eyes searched into mine, reaching out, and they were as blue
as sea distance. He took my hand and shook it slowly, holding it a long time as is often the way in the Azores, then made
me drink wine with him. "Wait," he said, and wriggled away
and was back in a minute to push into my hands, neatly
wrapped, half a slab of *massa cevada*.

Outside, the night was soft and clear and cool after the
crowded companionship of the café, and all along the road
the people waited. The road was spread with cypress boughs,
a thick soft odorous carpet strewn with flowers; arches of
green boughs were over the road. The procession was to come

this way, and then there was the sound of it, coming up the rise of road in the dark, the band playing the rather haunting, plaintive music that is always played at Espirito Santo. Now there was the band, leading the procession, dark against a nimbus of light behind; they came slowly, moving to the lulling cadence of the music. They came abreast of us, treading the green carpet soundlessly, blue gold-faced coats and white trousers, and behind them were the children. The children, little girls, all in white, were in two files, either side of the road; each, lost in the dream of it, carried a lantern. Between them, in the middle, was the priest; on a cushion he bore the silver crown, the silver crown of Espirito Santo. The beauty of it was hardly to be borne.

The enchantment had gathered and accumulated, and we went to the car dreamlike, not conscious of our legs. As we were getting in, about to go, there was a cry. It was the old whaler, running up the road to us, distressed, carrying something wrapped. I must forgive him, he said, please forget his discourtesy; he took from me the half-slab of *massa cevada* he had given me, then pressed upon me his packet. In it was a whole slab of *massa cevada.*

The Azoreans, it may be guessed, would have been devout people anyway, with the simple acceptance that must belong to remote island people whose context of life is bounded by inescapable and often dangerous simplicities. But for the Azoreans the normal island hazards are added to, overshadowed by, the constant sense of the sperm whale. For the Azores the sperm whale could well be a symbol; the consciousness of it permeates life, and piety becomes a needed assurance.

In those waters there are other whales—most species indeed are there—but it is only to the sperm whale that it is practical to apply the methods of open-boat whaling; the other species are too quick. They do not round out at the

Angra do Heroísmo, ingenuously beautiful, lies under the volcanic heights of Terceira.

The Walkiria, *moored in the harbor at Horta, with* Cetaceo *beyond.*
Burnt Mountain looms above. ¶*The bay of Porto Pim lies under*
Burnt Mountain; beyond, the land lifts away to the cratered crown
of Fayal. In the foreground the whale factory shows from behind the
stand of Arundo donaz. ¶*Nossa Senhora da Guia is the whalemen's*
own church and a whaling lookout as well.

IV

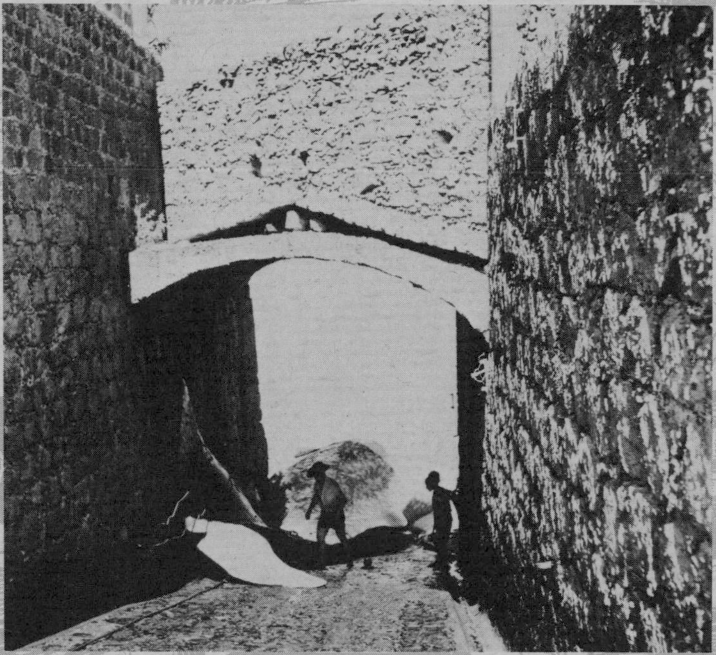

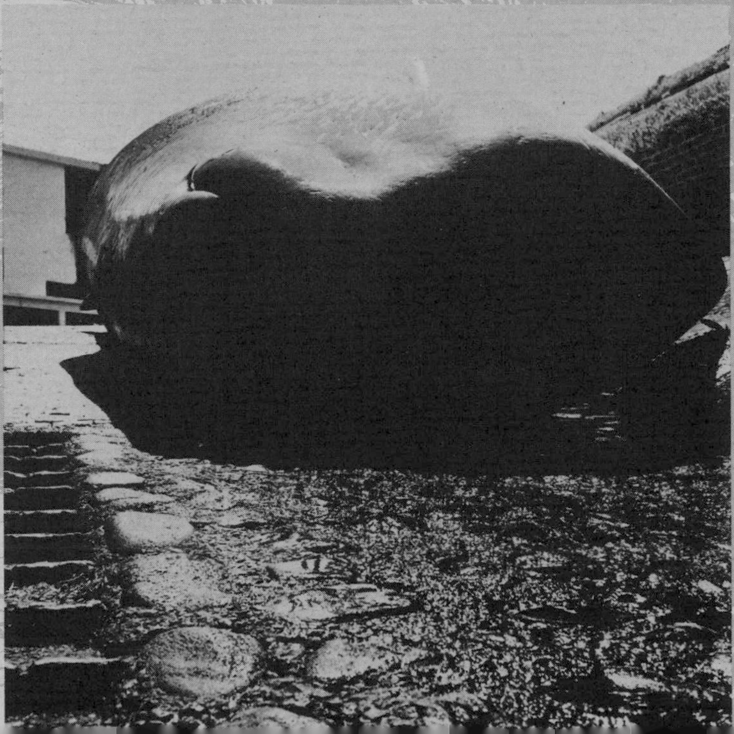

The whale, stranded at the slip of the factory at Porto Pim, is drawn slowly up the stones, lubricated with the fat and blood of a previous whale, to rest on the flensing platform. In the photograph at the lower left, the blowhole of the whale can be seen to the left.

Before the whale has fully stopped its haul onto the flensing platform, a cutting spade has begun the severance of head from trunk.

The cutting spade makes, near the mouth of the whale, a mortice through which a chain is fastened to draw the head aside to a corner of the flensing platform for separate working up. ¶One man with cutting spade chops through the blubber; another, with a blubber hook, is ready to drag it away.

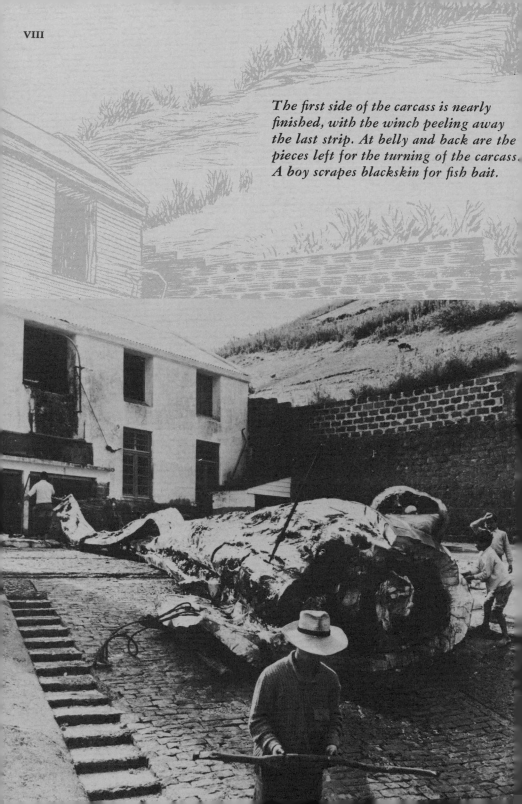

The first side of the carcass is nearly finished, with the winch peeling away the last strip. At belly and back are the pieces left for the turning of the carcass. A boy scrapes blackskin for fish bait.

surface in a leisurely way as the sperm whale does; so it is just the sperm whale, the *cachalote*, that fans those men to heats of adventure, abides with them as a constant fear.

It is as formidable a quarry as it could be. Though it is not as immense as the blue whale, which may be a hundred feet and even more, it is the biggest of the toothed whales (whales are all members of one or the other of two kinds, baleen whales and toothed whales). A sperm bull will grow to sixty feet and, rarely, to sixty-five feet; a cow will attain forty feet. It is a huge and ponderously dangerous creature.

Although the enormous lateral flukes of its tail are the whalers' greatest danger, its teeth, at times, are as terrible. Set in the lower jaw only, they are of variable number and are conical, not unlike the canine teeth of dogs but blunter, huge. They are seizing rather than chewing teeth, apt for catching and holding the slippery body of their main prey, the giant squid. In the lightless depths, far from sun and surface, there must be grim encounters; the sperm's great head is invariably scarred by tentacle-inflicted wounds. But however morose the fight, it must be assumed that the whale wins and then swallows its prey. The squids are three to four feet mostly, but they may be exceedingly big. Robert Clarke records being present at Porto Pim when a squid was taken from the stomach of a whale; the squid was 34 feet, 5 inches long and weighed 405 pounds.[2] There is evidence, he suggests, that such meals may not be altogether uncommon, and that the story of Jonah must be looked at less incredulously than has been supposed. A gullet that can engulf such monsters should not be incapable of accommodating a man —even if a man lacks the lubricosity of a squid.

The danger to the whalers in their frail craft, however,

[2] *Robert Clarke, "Sperm Whales of the Azores,"* Discovery Reports, *Vol. 28 (Cambridge, England: Cambridge University Press; 1956), p. 157.*

comes mainly from the thrashing of the whale at the harpooning, the lancing, or in the death throes—from the
incidental and not deliberately aggressive down-smash of
the enormous tail. The sperm whale does not, usually, turn
to conscious aggression; but the exceptions have been enough
to make a fearsome history.

BALEIA!

Of such a whale, ferocious by intent, I heard one evening when talk turned to whaling in Café Sport. It was from Pico the whaleboats had gone out, Peter said, and, soon, one of them darted its harpoon and fastened the whale. But the whale did not sound, did not burn out the whale line in the first frantic rush of the nearly invariable pattern; it flung itself upon the boat, smashing it. A second boat, standing by,

came in now and it too harpooned the whale, and upon it too the whale turned its assault, smashing it. Now a third boat came in and, as it darted its harpoon, the whale came upon it with jaws open wide. The awful chop of them shattered the *canoa* at the bows; then, Peter said, it went the length of the boat, chop, chop, chop, crushing to splinters its slender timbers.

Even by sheer inadvertence the teeth may be a means of disaster. On the afternoon of July 1, 1966, three whales were sighted eleven miles off São Mateus, which is on the south side of Pico, and, in the evening, a big whale was harpooned. When its initial runs had slackened, as it began to tire, it was lanced, then lanced again twice. The whalers were preparing for the kill. As they came in, as a fourth lance was thrown (and this is always a moment of the most searing hazard), the whale turned suddenly and the flail of its great flipper caught the *canoa*. The boat was badly damaged and three of the crew were tossed into the sea; of these one was the harpooner, José Silveira Jorge. He, as he must, was standing in the bows at that time, and was thrown into the side of the whale's open mouth, falling on the lower jaw. The teeth gripped his side in the flesh between ribs and pelvis; it was by hardly credible good fortune that the teeth did not penetrate and rupture the bowels. Those of the crew still in the damaged *canoa* now cut the line, and as the whale sheered away, sounded, and was lost, the men in the water were rescued. José Silveira Jorge was taken to Horta hospital, suffering from shock and a deep gash.

When so much in Azores whaling has come by inheritance from the old New Englanders, it is not surprising that in the Azores, as in Nantucket and New Bedford, the folk art of scrimshaw—that minor but often delightful art of decorating whale teeth—is practiced. The teeth are carved, sometimes into objects of quaintness, sometimes into ones of use—ash trays now are a common product, though in the past such things as pie-crust crimpers were common. Often the teeth, intact, are decorated by incising or painting. In Angra, on the island of Terceira, I came upon a couple, man and wife, who had painted a series of teeth with portraits of all the Presidents of the United States, a graceful little acknowledgment of inheritance. On each tooth was lettered, neatly, minutely, impeccably, an extract from a speech of the portrayed President.

It is from an organ in the queer huge head that the sperm whale takes its name. It has a fantastic shape, this head, square-ended in profile, immense, a third of the length of the whole huge beast, with a mouth strangely, almost ridiculously, incongruous. That mouth is nothing but practical— like, for example, the interesting absurdity of an anteater's. The whale's long, oddly narrow lower jaw, with its palisade of teeth that fit into the matching, toothless hollow of the upper jaw, is extremely efficient for gripping its slippery prey. Just above the mouth, under the towering bulk of head, is the eye, and it, like so much of the head, seems crowded, displaced, to make room for what is the greater contents of the head, the spermaceti organ.

The case, the New Englanders called it (*queize*, the Azoreans call it), is a great reservoir that holds the spermaceti. It is a light waxy oil, higher in quality than blubber oil and formerly of higher commercial value—now, at least on Fayal, it is not saved separately. Below the case is the junk (*janco* in Azorean), and it too, in its compartmented interior, has spermaceti. The purpose of the spermaceti organ can only be guessed, but it appears to be associated with the sperm whale's prodigious capacity for diving to the lightless depths where it finds its prey. The hollows that run laterally along the side of the head are roughly coincident with the division between the case above and the junk below. How great is the capacity of the case is shown by a large whale's yield of ten or more barrels of spermaceti—even, exceptionally, more than fifteen. As this sperm oil is ladled out when the case is broached, it is a pale straw-colored liquid; exposure to air turns it soon to a soft, solid, waxy white.

Dark gray you might call the sperm whale, but that would be unfair to its color, and even more to its texture. It is a deep, rather leaden color, with a hint of blue, but that is illuminated by its texture, a smooth, subtly plastic surface, inviting to the touch, such a sheeny delicacy of surface in so great a beast, unexpectedly thin. This is the "black-skin," or as the Azoreans call it, *blequesquine*. Only in very few sperm whales is the color uniform over the entire body; most have at least some white, invariably on the undersurface—the belly or lower jaw; and, quite often, there is mottling, gray and white, on the belly. I have heard, in

the Azores, of more generously piebald whales, with white straying up from the undersurface; but never did I find a witness to a whale of complete albinism.

Along the back of the whale, about its middle, there rises what might be called its dorsal fin; the old whalers' name for it, the hump, is more appropriate, and the Azoreans preserve it still; *ampo* they call it. It and the lesser ones of variable number behind it have more the smooth solidity of shapes on high hilltops, weather-worn to sculptured smoothness. "Fin" suggests something membranous; these lumps are broad from side to side—and of course they came to their shape much as the ancient hills, weathered smooth, came to theirs. Through the millions of generations that passed to form the species, the molding pressure of passage through water shaped them.

In former days ambergris was a rich prize, a rare bonus for the whalemen rather than a reckoned product of the whale; it was something that could, if its quality was high, command a high price for its use in perfumery. Now, though it has some value still, much of its former preciousness has been taken from it by modern synthetics. It is found in the hind gut of the sperm whale (and in no other whale), and in the Azores it is sought only in male whales. The belief, the tradition, that it may be found only in the male goes back beyond the reach of knowledge.

When it had its old high value, the hope of it must have colored every whaler's sortie. There was a man once, a man of Horta, who was walking the gritty strand under Burnt Mountain, between the town and Monte da Guia. He saw a roundish object floating in the smooth water of Porto Pim bay. He waded out, brought it to the shore. It was a great ball of ambergris; to him then it was a sudden fortune.

A T R A C K , a loose tread of feet, goes from the straggling edge of Horta and under the cindery pile of Burnt Mountain. You come out of the town, under the wall where the dog hangs over threatening with slavering fangs, down the slip of porous volcanic stone, and you are on Porto Pim beach, where the track is. It clings against the loose disintegrating margin of Burnt Mountain and skirts the beach; and as you walk, the sand, the dark sulky grit, filters into your shoes. It was very quiet there that Sunday, my first Sunday in Fayal, and across the smooth blue arc of the bay the whale factory glowed white against the olive fall of Monte da Guia, almost a shimmer in the thin sea light. Coming to the factory there was a butchery litter on the beach; bones, amorphous fragments, washing in the tide's edge, scattering on the sand. Above the tide marks, beautiful among the knacker's litter, there were clumps of a succulent plant, fat beds of glaucous triangular-sectioned leaves crowned with bold yellow or pink flowers. There, close to the factory, the smell lay on the air, that sickly, oily, sweetish whale-factory smell that, once known, does not quite leave the memory.

Places that often know great activity become ghostly when deserted, and the factory had a still silence, a haunted vacuity. The sloven's waste of whitened bones and spongy detritus outside did not pass the gate; inside it was clinical, everything neat—the great boilers, the marshaled stacks of faya wood. The afternoon light filtered in and lay mellowly on the massive tackles that maneuver the whale's bulk. The silent spell of inactivity was on the place, rather like midweek-empty churches in the country; there was an impulse to tread softly, speak in muted voice.

The flensing platform lay outside, built into the high flank of Monte da Guia, walled in; on the other side a wall dropped to the beach and the quiet water of the bay. Against the building, facing the flensing platform's slope, there were

the ponderous steam winches with massive chains and hooks. The platform's surface was smooth, guttered to drain blood away to settling tanks; the slip fell away, cobbled, steeply down and under the arch by the water.

The water was so still and green, such a peace lay on the place, that it seemed a relic of old and long-gone use; it seemed an impossibility that such an enormity of butchery could belong to its present. The cattle looked down from the little hanging fields above and moaned and mumbled with the soporific summery sound that cattle have, and when, soon, I went out of the factory, on the footpath above, there was a drowsy pulse of insects; small meadowy flowers bloomed there, and there was an infinity of placidity. But, I saw then, the tiny pastures and little fields of corn had fencing posts of whale jawbone. So you may often see bone of the sperm whale on Fayal, in incongruous uses. You may see doorframes of bone, and machine belts will sometimes have ties of bone in preference to metal; it is stronger, you will be told.

Next day the Sabbatical spell had dissipated; expectancy was back and I must go to the office of the Captain of the Port. Norberto, who went with me, said I must sign a form; in the office it was produced and translated for me. Norberto was apologetic. No one, he said, may go to sea with the whalers unless first he signs the form; by signing he absolves all but himself of responsibility for his safety. "It is very dangerous," Norberto said with an apologetic shrug and a lift of the eyebrows. I suppose the form has its cool official title, but in Horta it is usually called "the death warrant." I signed it and was given my copy.

Now I had the freedom of the hunt, now I could go as the whalers go. "Be on the quay at quarter to six in the morning," they said, and at five o'clock next morning I was persuading a reluctant digestion to accept at least some coffee. In the cool clear early light I walked the town's frontage on the sea, along the Avenida, past Café International and the old Spanish fort and down to the harbor. The towboat lay there against the quay, among the fishing boats bringing ashore the night's catch. It was cool and I shivered a little, though perhaps it was tension, not temperature, that made me do so. Abilio tended the engine; soon it burst into a deep throb of life, and now José Eugénio, who was skipper, and José Vicente were aboard. Now, soon, I thought, the call will come, the alarm; we will go to sea, the adventure will begin.

So, in my expectancy, I thought; but that is not the way of it. The engine was switched off; Abilio crouched over the radio. He was calling up the lookouts, the *vigias*, those watching posts on their cliff-edge aeries; he was signaling them with a two-note whistle, up and down. There was the answering call, the whistle. It was six o'clock and no whales sighted. Thus it is done every half-hour, the launch calling the lookouts at Salão, at Varadouro, at seven points around the island, each place having an arc of vision largely overlapping those on either side. So, simultaneously, the whole plain of ocean is scanned, searched for the blow of a whale, the low arching blow that is characteristic of the sperm whale. On days of poor visibility, poor whaling days, the reach of vision may be only four or five miles, but when the weather is clear it may be twenty-five miles.

This was such a day, a day that justified the cold prickle of expectation, and at half-past six there was the calling whistle again, and again there was no whale sighted. It was early in the season, they said and shrugged, only May; the full abundance of whales comes in June. But two whales had been caught the previous day; who knows, there may be whales today—and, at seven o'clock, when the call was made again, there was the electrifying, nerve-twanging word, *baleia*. A lookout at Castelo Branco had sighted a blow, and I, tautly strung, thought, now is the searing moment. But, as the seconds passed, there was nothing more, nothing but whistle and question and answer, and it was explained that the blow was too far off. We must wait, they said; perhaps the whale will move in, come within a distance that makes it practical to chase. The span of a day does not give time to chase and kill a too-far-off whale, and not be benighted by darkness in the frail vulnerability of the whaleboats.

So we waited and I, as you will at such times of tension, fell to absent scrutiny of the myriads of tiny fish in the green water against the boat. They came, a million strong, passing and repassing, while a loose strand of my chained attention speculated on the form of their regular beat; their comings, around and around, were like a metronome beating out time.

Now there was the radio again. It was the whaling headquarters in Horta; we must go to sea, out beyond Castelo Branco, out where another launch, *Cetacea*, lay with her tow of the two whales killed the previous day. The power of our launch, *Walkiria*, must be added to that of *Cetacea*. That whale had shown its blow no nearer; there was to be no whale, no chase and kill today, no fearsomely conjectured peril. The cold taut tension died, and I did not know if it was relief or frustration that I felt.

Walkiria throbbed to life, churned across the harbor, and we turned the mole and headed through the channel between Fayal and Pico, headed for sea at eighteen knots. The light had not lifted yet to full broad day; a coronet of cloud clung about the aspiring tip of Pico's peak, shining through with opalescent light. The sea, under the craggy tumble of Fayal's coast, again had the deep paintlike color, the deep, deep, blue—like pigment—because we were close in here, under the land's reflection. Pico receded under the port quarter and became a pinnacle of night-blue velvet with a chiffon hang of cloud on its summit.

We were bearing out now, out from Fayal; there was the long range of its coast with the skirted spread of old cold lava; it was chambered with an intricacy of caverns, open where the sea had shorn off the face of the rock. They were round-topped, these caves, shaped like bubbles, and the realization came suddenly that that is what they were, gargantuan gas bubbles left by the inconceivable seethe and simmer of the island's orgasmic birth. What enormity of eruption of earth's loins could have such scale, I wondered, and I looked at those men in the launch with me and thought that I sensed in them, under their quietness, some infection of the inward fire.

And now, two miles or so off, gauzy in the shimmer of emerging sun, lay *Cetacea*. She turned to substance as we came up on her, and then I saw, just away from her stern, two low blue-gray humps in the sea. These then were whales at last, sperm whales. I could see so little of them, barely awash above the surface; but their size, their weight, became obvious when we had tied up to *Cetacea* and the two launches together began to tow. Their power, together, could just make way, two knots perhaps. So we went, creeping, till we came to Porto Pim, into the still translucence under Monte da Guia.

There is a buoy there, a little off the slipway, and to it the whales were secured; I looked down, through the cool clarity of water under our keel, and there was the tail, the huge flukes, wide as the width of a room. A boat was coming out from the slip, a small sculled boat, bringing a light wire cable to secure to one of the whales; the wire came from a winch. So the whale was brought up to the slip, and as it stranded there, as the water became opaque with the thick red ooze of its blood, men and boys, bare-legged, waded around it, clustering like flies about its head. They had scrapers, sharpened and bent from slips of old iron, fastened to handles; they were scraping the head for blackskin, scraping off the oddly thin, almost membranous

skin for use as fishing bait.

Now men, barefooted, in shorts or with pantaloons rolled thigh-high, were laboring down the slipway, dragging the ponderous tackles from the winches. A heavy chain was fastened around the tail, in front of the flukes, and to that the tackles were secured. As the whale began to move slowly up the slip, as the winches steamed and labored, the boys

and men came too, still scraping blackskin. The whale went slowly, with a soft, shuffling, rustling sound on the cobbles of the slip, until it was at the top and on the easy slope of the flensing platform; it had not fully stopped when two men were at its head with cutting spades. They were working at once, with spare short economical movements, working with brief downward chops. The sound of it was soft, a chunky softness, like chopping into a soft apple; cutting either side, starting high up, they were making a circlet around the body.

As they went, the cut, almost surgically neat, opened a gape in the dark dull sheen of the blackskin, showing within the blubber, white with a faint rosy tint from the stain of blood. Thus far it did not seem bloody; the blubber looked like a confection, soft but firm, opening firmly to the cut, like white fondant or marshmallow. There was nearly a foot's thickness of the blubber, clean and white and sugary; but then they were through that, through to the tissues beneath, and suddenly the blood was gouting.

The blood flooded from the vast carcass as this grotesque butchery proceeded, running audibly, lapping the legs and feet of the men and flowing in the drainage gutters. Now a wire cable had been put to the head and from there to a smaller winch in the corner of the flensing platform; as the men continued chopping in, slowly the winch dragged, bending the head away from the trunk. With heavier cutting spades the spine was severed, and then, the main artery. The men were standing within the carcass, between head and trunk, chopping, chopping, and the torrent of blood from the big artery burst out, swirled through their legs till they were red to the thighs, ran in torrents through the gutters and down the slip, jumping from stone to stone. In the still water of the bay below the opaque red stain spread slowly.

Then the head was fully severed; the winch took its weight, drew it, shuffling on the cement of the platform, till it was drawn to the side, away from the carcass. Whaleboat men were there; they were to flense away the blubber, open the case, take out the spermaceti.

Meanwhile, flensing had advanced upon the main carcass; the men had made long cuts longitudinally along the body, but staggered upward and then along again so as to leave two sections of blubber—by the belly and by the back— to give a purchase for the tackles when the whale must be turned for working up the other side. Then downward cuts were made along the strips, cutting the blubber into two-foot sections. The boys took these, dragging them with iron blubber-hooks, leaning their small weight, straining small young muscles, dragging away the massive weight to feed the tall, vertical rank of great cookers within the building. There was a hoist at the back of the flensing platform; it lifted the blubber to a door, high up, which gave onto a platform serving the cookers.

As the work went on, this huge and bloody dismemberment, this apparently horrid disarray, I perceived in it a rhythm, a vast fluency. I saw that within the outrageous blood-paddling knacker's muck and slither there was a neat economy of working, a precise passage from stage to stage, an accumulation of experience that had come to a polish. The flanks were stripped of the blubber, the men outlining the strips, going neatly along with the soft chop chop of the cutting spades, then mortising a hole into the forward end of the strip to receive the hook from the winch. Then, as the winch drew on it with massive gentleness, lifting the strip, turning back the marshmallow blubber under the blackskin, the men came with it, easing it away from the opalescent sheen of the fascia beneath.

Soon, with such ponderous facility, the whole side of the whale had been stripped, all but the two pieces by back and belly for the turning; there it lay, ready for the butchering of the meat under the fascia. Last of all the flipper was removed, a man standing on the whale, chopping down into the joint.

The meat was taken from the belly first, taken in slabs by cutting spades. And then from the back, enormous fillets were stripped away by the winch's modulated power till all was gone and there were the naked ribs and the immensity of the organs within them. Then the ribs were taken, chopped free of the vertebrae and dragged by the winch, two at a time. So one side was finished, and now the carcass was turned, lifted over by wires toggled to those pieces of blubber left for that purpose. As that first side had been stripped, so was the other side. Only the bare backbone was left, that and the vast slither of the guts, that hill of viscera which was drawn, sliding, slipping, undulating, down the slip to the water. Later, it would be towed to sea.

The smell, that whale-factory smell, lay viscously on the air now; the factory was busy, the tall chimney smoking, the cookers stoked with faya wood, cookers for blubber and cookers for bone. The blubber would be rendered down to oil, the cooked bone dried and ground for bonemeal. The meat was being cut, first into lumps, then, at a trestle, into small cubes that would be dried, not cooked, and made into meal. The whaleboat men had finished their work on the head now; the skull was sawed up, the blubber flensed, the spermaceti taken. In earlier days the spermaceti had been jealously separated, saved apart for its finer quality, but not now; all—blubber-oil and spermaceti—is saved together. The lower jawbones had been put aside; from them, later, there would come the taking of the teeth, "stripping ivory," saving the teeth for scrimshaw.

I left the factory now, out past the towering cookers, out of the door; suddenly there was other air, no blood, no vast outrageous guts. There was the clean calm sea beyond the isthmus, the turn of little road winding the flank of Monte da Guia. I turned onto it, away from the factory, climbing away above the sea. Suddenly it was quiet and lonely and the air sweet with space.

5

TH IS WAS a small rough road, spiraling narrowly around the abrupt flanks of Monte da Guia, lifting quickly till all of Horta lay below, palely pink and beige and soft fondant green, a pale dapple between the blue sweep of sea and dark rumpled toss and pinnacle of hinterland. There was the scorched cindery pile of Burnt Mountain and the little waist of isthmus, and beyond that the blue arc of Porto Pim bay. The road hung over the sea against a precarious cling of tiny cultivated plots, hedged and held by the giant grass, *Arundo donax.* Above the road, on the right, the ground climbed up precipitously with a sort of impertinent defiance of natural law, plotted out in those tiny fields in their fences of *Arundo donax.* The neat crops grew there, and above that was the sharp tilt of pastures and the drowsing cattle.

Where now was the noisome blood and slither of the flensing platform, all those quaking guts? I could hear still, under the hill, the clank of the monstrous tackle, but with a soft summery muffle now, merged with insect hum and birds' lilt. The road was steep and slow to climb in the spangled gauze of sunny air, and at a turn hung dizzily above the sea, I paused. There was a sigh of distant surf, a murmur; it was so still, so warm, the sea so jewel-blue that the whale factory had become a queer dream of other times immeasurably removed. There across the five-mile straits was Pico, soaring to its sublime peak and with no veiling wisp of cloud, almost diaphanous, a translucency of smoky mauve and murmurous blue. A yacht had tacked up the straits and waited now, a mile offshore, for the pilot boat; I saw it, minute and black, come alongside, imagined the pilot going aboard, and it was like watching toys, insects, something infinitely reduced from human scale. To see it so, a sort of tiny mime, heightened the sense of lofty sunny aerial loneliness, that kind of bliss that can come in such places.

I was above the gardens now, above the pastures, climbing and winding around the upflung sides of Monte da Guia, free of blood and butchery, free of all, free almost of earth—were that not a blasphemy when earth can be so much a heaven. The road still climbed on, climbing in brief, straight stretches, then turning abruptly around a shoulder of hill in the blue shimmer of air above the sea. There were still small fields, but most of the tumble of the hill now was faya and giant heather, rough growth molded over the rumple of volcanic rock—because Monte da Guia, so tranquil now, is a dead volcano.

Then, just off from a sharp elbow of the road, there was the tiny church, smaller almost than a church could ever be, the whalers' church of Senhora da Guia. Steps went up to it, where it stood within a low-walled terrace, perched there, aerie-fashion, above the vast sublimity of ocean; it is so sited because it is also a lookout. Its vestry contains not symbols of sanctity, but a radio for communication with the two launches and the whaling headquarters in Horta. I walked past the door, past the vestry, and there, behind the church and looking over the sea, was Eduino. Eduino is a lookout man.

He sat astride a sort of trestle seat; the seat was three feet or so long, and at its forward end there was a vertical neck. On that, at eye level, binoculars were fixed vertically, but adjustable by a thumbscrew to turn laterally so that their arc could scan that whole sweep of sea. There, for all his hours of duty, Eduino sits, as others sit at the other six lookouts round Fayal's coast, searching the enormous oceanic prospect for the blow of a whale. A taxing, meticulous scrutiny it must be, so it seemed to me; such a vastness of sea—all glint and ruffle—in which to find a minute distant whale's blow. Some whales have a high, obvious blow, but the sperm whale's is low and arching, though it is often repeated many times before the whale sounds again.

On the column that carried the binoculars there was, as well, a compass; thus, when a single blow, or the blows of a school of whales is seen, a bearing can be taken and given to the tow launches. All this Eduino, who was a friendly man, told me. "Sit there," he said, "look through the glasses —perhaps you will see a *baleia*." And sit there I did and scanned the huge plain of sea, but nothing could I see but the endless recessions of waves. From first light Eduino had been there, and till about four o'clock so he would be still, methodically sweeping the sea for the tiny distant plume that meant, perhaps, sixty feet of sperm whale. Sometimes, he said, a whale would be close in, three miles, but more often it would be farther; on good days he could see a blow twenty-five miles out and on exceptional days, thirty or more miles. Clear windless weather is best whaling weather; the days least liked are those with a vague hang of moisture, diffused days, and they come often in the Azores.

Any day that a whale may be sighted and that a boat may be launched from the shore, the whalers will go to sea; but it is a succession of still fine days, summery days, that gives good whaling, and, because summer brings the main concentration of whales in Azorean waters, June, July, August, and September are the best months for whaling. It is then that the high tense expectancy hangs over Horta. But because the chance of a whale is never entirely gone, the *vigias* are manned throughout the year.

I was to learn that Eduino's *vigia*, that simple lonely lookout by the little church, was not typical of all. Others are more elaborate, bigger, built of stone faced with con crete; the watchers, and there may be three, sitting within with binoculars trained through a long opening from which a shutter lifts up. I saw a smaller one, westward along the coast, toward the new volcano, that stood beside the road and on the brink of an awesome scarp that fell to the sea. Perhaps it could take two men, though I suspect but one, but it too was solid with stone and concrete like the bigger ones. So indeed they must be; the rocky pinnacles of the islands receive all the wild midwinter fury of the Atlantic.

Early in the day, soon after first light, before the sun rises to put a dazzle on distances, about six o'clock, is the best time for the raising of a whale. On a good day the light is, though low, very clear and defined; it is then, so the records show, that most whales are seen. This is providential for the whalemen; their constant dread, too often justified, is that the fall of night shall come upon them many miles offshore in circumstances of great danger. There, in such a lonely immensity of sea, weather is immeasurably variable, unpredictable, and light of day is at least some insurance against peril that, in changing degree, is always there.

Senhor Tomas Alberto de Azevedo told me a story, and though memory no longer holds all its details, its grim theme cannot be dislodged. There was a day when whales were raised and boats put to sea; there was a launch whose engine-man was Eduardo Serafim. The launch towed two *canoas*, and with them on this occasion went a fishing boat; its skipper was José Faidoça. They had been at sea two hours when the launch's engine failed, and all the striving of Eduardo Serafim would not bring life to it; as he worked the weather worsened, threatening storm. Time passed and

they drifted and Eduardo fought desperately to wake the engine; then abruptly the storm was on them. The sky lowered and blackened, the seas mounted and spumed; they lay helplessly in the storm's attack.

One of the *canoas* with its seven men cast off from the launch, setting off to bring help. They never reached land. They came within sight of it, terribly, tormentingly close; they were within half a mile of the shore, in the sight of their families waiting for them. But they could come no closer. There, under the eyes of their families, the boat foundered; all seven men were lost. Still, now, the weeping and despair of those on shore is fresh in the mind of Tomas Alberto.

Meanwhile those in the other *canoa*, Eduardo in the launch, and the fishing-boat skipper, after hours under the lash of the storm, decided they must abandon all but the fishing boat; only in it was there chance for survival. They cut loose the *canoa* and its crew went aboard the fishing boat; Eduardo Serafim would not come aboard—he could not, he said. He was tormented by a sense of responsibility; it was the failure of his engine, he said, which had brought such crisis upon them all. He must stay with the launch; he felt himself inescapably tied to the fate of it, whatever that might be. So he stayed aboard the launch, and the fishing boat made such way as it could to reach shore. What happened to it in the awful hours of that voyage I do not know, but when, eventually, it did make land at Faja Ros Viames, only three survivors were aboard.

Eduardo, left alone, abandoned himself to the sea's wild whim, helplessly waiting. He did put overboard a mooring stone on a rope, lowering it to drag and so give, perhaps, a shred of stability to the launch; but there was no more he could do. He had no food, but by great good fortune he had water. So, drifting in the storm-driven heave and hiss of the sea, he went all night, all the next day, and through another night. When dawn seeped through on the third day, gray, dark, and lugubrious, he still lay in the sea's huge wallow; but the storm was abating, the wind lessening. So the morning went till midday, and now hope had revived in him;

at the morning's end the mist cleared suddenly, and there, ahead by some miles, was land. It was directly in the line of his drift, and at last he came to shore. He had come to Porto Judea on the island of Terceira, fifty miles from his embarkation.

That grim story should not suggest that all raising of whales comes so early in the morning or that the whalers will not put to sea for a later sighting or, indeed, that they are not often overtaken by night while still at sea; I have been so overtaken myself. Nor should it be thought that disaster is an inevitable corollary of the fall of night. But night is an enhancement of the constant danger; the whalers will avoid it if they can. Thus the watch of the *vigias* is usually only till about four o'clock or perhaps a little later—though, right to the end, till four o'clock or after, if a whale is raised the boats will put to sea. The cry *"Baleia! Baleia!"* acts like adrenaline, instantly rousing the passion, the half-madness; at that cry all other considerations cease.

Even there, on the little terrace of Senhora da Guia alone with Eduino, in the lofty sunny serenity so far above the sea, I had some sense of this. I could imagine how, should we see the minute white thistle-shape of a whale's blow, so small a thing in that vast peace of sea, it would crackle through Horta below, go like a shock through there and through the boat stations. In an instant it would turn all those men from desultory inconsequentialities to a community of passion.

I left Eduino, left him at his scrutiny, and walked slowly down the fall of narrow road. The birds sang, butterflies fluttered to brief resting, and the whole high sunny place was drowsy with summer peace. Because it was past the middle of the day, about one o'clock, I climbed up from the road and up the bank to sit just within the falling face of a little field. Here I could eat the lunch I had brought in case the rocket's call should take me to sea to chase a whale. White climbing roses, some garden escape, had established themselves here. The fragrant rampant tangle ran both ways from me, wholly possessing the bank to my eyes' limit, to the road's turn, up and down. In the field, against the roses, there was a stand of bracken, and the aromatic scent of it drawn by the sun merged with the roses' fragrance. Such peace, such enchantment, made of the rough red wine and the bread and cheese a sort of bliss. And, I suppose, it was intensified by the unadmitted consciousness that this was a consoling interlude before the peril that was inevitably to come.

Horta lay below, almost too perfectly lovely and pastel-pale to be real, a gentle dazzle of icing-sugar color between the dark olive of the heights and the sea's deep blue. And there to the left was Porto Pim, the horseshoe sweep of bay, limpid-smooth, deep aquamarine. But not all of it was so; directly below me was the whale factory, and on its flensing platform there were tiny figures still busy at their butchery. They had nearly finished the working up of the second whale. From the bottom of the slip the bloody smear had spread; now, solid red, opaque, it had engulfed at least an acre of the blue placidity. There then was the reminder of what my business in Fayal was; there, suddenly, was the end of bliss. I got up, scrambled to the road; but still as I went slowly down, there was a remnant of the enchantment. The air still sang, the butterflies still flirted in the flowers, Horta was as beautiful. Why, I asked myself, should I not enjoy this lovely present? Tomorrow or the next tomorrow might bring anything.

When tomorrow came, and in the early glimmer of light between dawn and sunrise I walked along the Avenida against the sea, under the tall palms in the square and down to the harbor, the sequence was as before. Abilio was at his engine and, at six o'clock, the radio round of the lookouts started. The start of the day was calm but overcast, and with a threat of wind; as the time of sunrise came— though there was no sun to be seen—the wind came too, a ruffle first then growing and jostling the trees by the harbor. The men on the quay raised skeptical eyes to the sky; there was a shaking of heads, a pursing of mouths, a lifting of shoulders, a spreading of hands.

"No *baleia* today," they said. "There was rain in the night, and now the wind—wind is no good for *baleia*; in wind they go far off. Wind is bad, rain is bad. Calm, sunny weather is best for *baleia*—then they are much at the surface." And, they told me, when the wet windy overcast weather comes it is likely to stay for five days. "But," they added, being friendly men who wished me to be happy, "who knows, it may die overnight—sometimes it does."

So I must wait, and waiting was painful; when you are keyed to dangerous adventure, raised to its high nervous pitch, postponement induces an ennui, a sort of nervous paralysis. I watched the tiny fish, millions again, still at their parading, coming and going and coming and going and seeming to mark off unused time. Death came marauding among them once, a raiding giant, a red fish a full nine inches long; it wheeled and slashed through the tiny prey, scattering them. Then the attacker had gone, the patrolling millions had formed up again, and that momentary incident had passed into forgetfulness. Minute fish preyed upon by little fish; little fish preyed upon by bigger fish; and so on and so on to men, relatively tiny, preying upon the great whales; the universal pattern runs its cycle, all fits into all, and balance is maintained. Or so it is unless man, too clever, makes deadly machines for his predation, contaminates environments, throws coarse destruction into the delicate precision of ecology.

The heavy hours passed, and at the halves of each the routine radio round of the *vigias* was made; but expectancy had gone. There was relief when, at one o'clock, it was acknowledged that there would be no whales today.

When the last hours before darkness came, I went to Salão, the whaleboat station along the north coast. A *canoa* had been overhauled at the whaling headquarters in Horta; now, repaired and repainted, it must be returned to Salão and another brought back for overhaul. In the harbor, in the launch *Walkiria*, we took in tow the *canoa*, elegant, pristine-pretty in new paint—white hull and yellow strake, the colors of Fayal. With me in the launch's stern was José Rufino, a whaleboat skipper, lean and brown and gentle-mannered, a swart handsome man who had been a great harpooner till he had been promoted to captain—or, in whaling usage, boatheader—promoted from bows to stern. The Azorean term for boatheader is *mestre.*

Walkiria's throttle roared, we swept across the harbor, past the mole and out to sea, rounding the coast and the black harsh jut of headland, running under that ferociously hostile coast with the *canoa* riding like a sea bird in our wake. We rode the high gray swell, over the creaming tattered tops and into the lurching troughs, elated with sea and wind and broken sky, and I wondering how there could be launching or landing anywhere. There was no interval in the restless surly crash and tumble of the surf under the sheer fall of cliff.

Walkiria surged on, rounded a last headland, and ahead in the boil of sea, close-in, the other *canoa* waited, lifting and dancing and bucketing feather-fashion on the heave and lash against the jagged pile of rock under the cliff. So she appeared at a distance, light and dancing; coming close I saw that her crew strove with the sea, holding her there, lest the sea dash her frail timber on the rock. The cliff's top was lower, a little dipped from the dizzy heights beyond, but under the cliff the pile of rock had so menacing and jagged a tumble, the surf flung and towered so fiercely, that landing or launching did not seem possible. Then I saw that a slip zigzagged from cliff's top to sea, wrought into the rock. Still there seemed to me no way of maneuvering these long and bucking boats through the frantic toss of sea.

Walkiria hove to now, drew up the towed *canoa* on its cable, and José Rufino went aboard her, went aft, and took the long steering oar; others from *Walkiria* went aboard and took paddles. Then, while they held her in the plunging sea, the other *canoa* came up so close that I thought she must be smashed against *Walkiria*. But, with the boatheader throwing his weight on the steering oar, the crew paddling to his orders just audible above the surf's uproar, they brought her in with the precision of a chessman till her rope could be thrown to the launch and she fastened in tow. Now the *canoas* were maneuvered toward each other and, as I watched without belief, the crews transferred in all that chaotic boil of sea and José and the others came aboard *Walkiria* again. And how, I wondered, will they take that boat ashore, how will they strand her on that slip so besieged by the beating sea? But they took her, bearing at an angle to the slip, and the boatheader at the critical moment thrusting out with all his weight on the long steering oar; so she came, gently at last, with a miraculous precision, gently grounding on the slip. So beautiful had all this boatwork been, so controlled, so certain, that it had a cadence.

Fayal has two boat stations—Salão, commanding the

island's northern arc of ocean, and Varadouro on the south-
ern coast. At Varadouro I never saw more than one boat, and
it stranded on the open beach, though tucked under a high
precipice and kept under roof-shaped covers. There it lies, as
the whaleboats always lie, with all its gear aboard, always
ready for the instant call to sea. There was not, formerly, a
boat station at Varadouro; it had been at Capelo, at the
island's western end, close to the point at Capelinhos. Capelo had been a whalemen's community; they had their
cottages and their gardens and the whaleboats were there.
So it was until 1958; then the new volcano erupted, and
Capelo was buried. All you may see now are the roofless
skeletons of those few whalers' cottages that are not under
the ashy red desert left by the volcano.

The open-beach launching at Varadouro seems to explain the only significant difference between the old New
England whaleboats and those of the Azores. Those of New
England were never more than thirty feet long, and, probably, a majority were twenty-eight feet; but these were
ship's boats—they had to be accommodated aboard and
they had to be lowered and hoisted. As it was their keels
were supported during lowering and hoisting, and even so,
had they been much longer, so light was the timber in
them they could have broken their backs or at least sprung
their planks.

The Azores boats have no such limitation; they are
launched from slip or beach and thus are able to have that
greater length which allows one more crewman. There were
six in a Yankee boat; the Azores boat, usually thirty-seven or
thirty-eight feet long, has a crew of seven. Beyond that
differences are slight; the tradition of building, like that of
the words used, has come little changed from the New
Englanders to the Azoreans. The Azorean boats are carvel-

built—smooth-skinned, that is—and so, latterly, were the Yankee boats. Clinker building, originally used on New England boats, must, almost beyond doubt, have been abandoned because the lapping of water against the staggered strakes is so much more noisy than it is against a smooth hull—and there is no firmer canon of whalemen than that the sperm whale has acutely sensitive hearing. Both Yankee and Azorean show the same enchanting grace of line, the same derivation from canoes, with rounded bottom and pointed bows and stern. The stern is pointed, like the bows, because in the instant after the throw or thrust of harpoon or lance the boat must back water to clear the danger of the whale's upflung mighty tail or its thrashing flippers.

Never, of course, have I seen one of the old New England boats; but a mind's eye picture of them suggests that lovely of line as they were, the longer Azorean boat is even more so—such is the nature of these craft that greater length enhances.

Chasing a whale may be by pulling on the long oars or by sailing, and the later Yankee boats, to increase sail area, adopted the centerboard. Azorean whaleboats have no centerboard—perhaps because the boats are dragged up on pebbly beaches. But, with or without a centerboard, the spread of canvas on an Azorean boat is enormous for so slight, light, and shallow a craft—six feet eight inches in the beam, two feet six inches in depth. In Horta they told me that were a *canoa* to have its sails hoist without the crew aboard it would capsize at once, and I still remember sharply the first time I was at sea with the whalers and the mast was stepped and then the sails hoist. I could not help but be apprehensive that even if the boat did not capsize immediately, the first touch of wind would cause it to. As it was we, the crew and I, had to lean well out to windward and, when we went about, go as one man to the other gunwale. To gain every possible inch of mainsail, the gaff is peaked right up, high above the mast.

The planking of the *canoas*, which I took to be some sort of pine, is, so they told me in Fayal, imported from America. It is half an inch thick. The timber used for the ribs is local; it is called *acacear amarella*, which is a species of acacia and very hard.

The intrinsic beauty of Azores whaleboats is enhanced by the mode of painting. The hull is white, and though it may be guessed that this has the practical justification of being less obvious from below than a darker color would be, in the characteristic Portuguese fashion a decorative virtue is made of it; combined with that white hull is the top strake of bright color, the color being a declaration of the boat's island of origin. A Pico boat has blue, a clear cobalt; a Fayal boat has yellow with a gunwale of red; São Jorge has green. The pretty gaiety of that winsome flair cannot be contained; it has its little evidences throughout the boat. I saw many most beguilingly painted inside with pink, and I have seen boats whose name on the quarter has been contained within a decorative white panel with a wreathing of carved and painted leaves. Some of the boat's furniture, such as gunwale strakes and cleats, are sometimes of turned and polished whalebone.

The ordering of the parts inside the boat follows closely its New England precursor. In the bows, at the top of the stem, there is a cleft, a channel; this is the chocks, a passage to contain the running out of the whale line. The chocks may have a metal roller, but those I have seen have been of plain wood, burnished nearly to satin by the running of the line. Immediately aft, within the swell of the bows, there is a triangular area, decked in and sunk below the level of the gunwales; this is the box, and its purpose is to hold those few fathoms of line directly fastened to the harpoon, the box line or box warp, the provider of a light slack between harpoon and main line.

At the after edge of the box, crossing the boat from gunwale to gunwale and flush with it, there is the clumsy cleat or thigh board, a stout plank that has in it a semi-circular notch, a little to port of center. It is in this notch that the harpooner braces his left thigh as he stands to dart the harpoon; it is said, though I have not seen it, that it may occa-

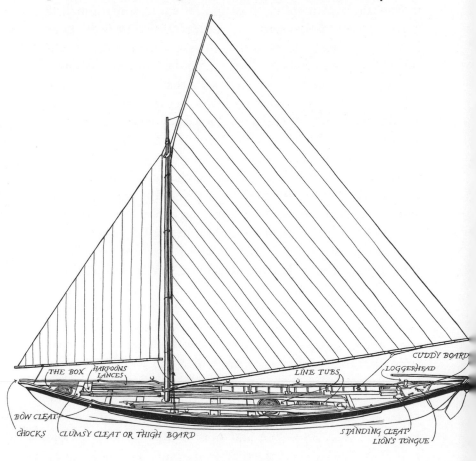

THE BOX · HARPOONS LANCES · LINE TUBS · CUDDY BOARD · LOGGERHEAD · BOW CLEAT · CHOCKS · CLUMSY CLEAT OR THIGH BOARD · STANDING CLEAT · LION'S TONGUE

sionally be located in the center for an ambidextrous harpooner, equally able to dart the harpoon with left or right arm.

Just a little aft of the clumsy cleat, and coming from as far aft as the mast, there is on either gunwale a robust fairlead that forms up there to make a forward-opening cleat. These are the bow cleats; they have several important functions, and of these one is "bowing on" a whale. When a fastened whale has reached that point in the fight when it is at least partially tired and ready for lancing, the straining line is taken from the chocks to a bow cleat so that the boat may be veered, otter-fashion, to tow parallel to the whale and thus favorably for coming in for lancing. Similarly the line may serve through a bow cleat when coming alongside a dead whale to prepare for towing it.

But there is another and more crucial purpose for the bow cleats, and it cannot be sharply perceived without knowing how deadly can be the running out of the line when a whale has been fastened. It burns out, pouring away along the midships line of the boat, and for a man to go foul of it may be (and so often has been) fatal. In the old New England boats there were devices against the line's kicking wild—the chock pin and the kicking strap. The first was a slender wooden peg passed laterally through the upper part of the chocks above the line, and the second was a piece of rope going from end to end of the clumsy cleat above the line. Neither is ordinarily used in Azores boats (though I have seen a chock pin), and a violently kicking line can jump the chocks. It is then that one or the other of the bow cleats catches it and prevents the appalling chance of its sweeping the length of the boat.

In the stern there is the cuddy-board, against which the skipper—boatheader—has his station, and there at quiet

times he has his seat. It is a decking-in of the last few feet
of the boat, flush with the gunwales; it carries the loggerhead, the most crucial single object in the playing and
subjection of a whale. This loggerhead is a bollard, about
eight inches high, narrow at the base and sloping out to a
wider diameter at the top. It provides the means of exerting
pressure on the whale; the line is payed out against the check
it makes, and line is recovered around it.

But before the line can come to the loggerhead it must
come from the line tubs; of those there are two, stowed
amidships between thwarts, one between the last, or after-
thwart, and the next, or tub-thwart; the other, forward
again, between the tub-thwart and line-thwart. Formerly
the tubs were always circular, cooper-built, and some still
are; but I have sailed in boats in which the tubs were
square. Each holds 120 fathoms of line. That is coiled down
with the most precise exactitude, because one coil going
foul could bring disaster to the boat during the first ferocious
rush of the whale.

The line comes first from the after-tub, going from there
to be taken around the loggerhead and then up the fore-and-
aft midline of the boat, between the oarsmen, to its attachment to the box line, which is in turn attached to the
harpoon. When the dart is made, when the harpoon has
gone home in the whale, the awful impetuosity of its first
run cannot be checked; it must have its way. But then the
run slows, stops, and the slackening line is given a turn or
two around the loggerhead. The fight goes on, the whale
tows the boat, and, as it does, the line is snubbed around
the loggerhead, or, as need comes, payed out. When at last
the whale tires, when the time comes for lancing and the
boat hauls up on the whale, the slack is brought in around
the loggerhead. All this the boatheader does, and as he

gathers the slack he coils it down before him on the short platform, just raised from the bottom timbers of the boat, on which he stands when not going on a whale.

To withstand such enormous stresses, the loggerhead is robustly built into the boat; it goes through the cuddy-board, down to the keel, into which it is inserted. Then to give it strength laterally as well as vertically, on the cuddy-board it passes through a king-plank—the lion's tongue or loggerhead strip—which, oddly curved, runs from the forward edge of the cuddy-board right into the point of the stern.

Immediately forward of the cuddy-board, fastened on the risings, halfway up the sides of the boat, there are two projections, one on either side, like short shelves a foot wide; they are the standing cleats. It is on these that the boat-header stands, straddling the boat, when going on a whale; he stands there so that, so elevated, his view is better. As often as not none aboard but the boatheader and the harpooner will see the whale before it is darted. He is also poised upon the standing cleats when using the great steering oar.

An Azorean whaleboat has six thwarts, differing from the Yankee boats which had five; their names, going aft, are harpooner-thwart, bow-thwart, midships-thwart, line-thwart, tub-thwart, after-thwart. From under the second thwart, forward, a platform goes over the bottom timbers similar to that on which the boatheader stands. On this forward platform the harpooner stands when, with thigh braced in the clumsy cleat, he darts the harpoon. It is also against the second thwart that the mast is stepped, and for that it is specially strengthened; the mast is there, against the forward edge of the thwart, in a hinged tabernacle, which allows the raising or lowering of the entire mast quickly and neatly. Such ease, such speed, is vital; when the boat has gone on a whale under sail, and the harpoon has been darted, mast and sails must be struck very quickly.

So it may be said, and, so said, it sounds simple; but this must be done in the fearsome crisis of the moments that follow the fastening of the whale. The mast is unstepped, lowered on its hinge, and, the stays and halyards having been first loosened, all is lowered aft. The mainsail is bundled, then jib, gaff, mast, and sail are lashed with the main sheet, and all stowed so as to lie over one quarter, clear of the running line. Just thus—but the line is kicking down the boat, pouring away from the instant the harpoon fastens, smoking down the length of a boat that is so cluttered that there seems not an inch to push a penny. In that situation the smallest failure in coolness, in trim efficiency in the heavy handling, could mean fouling the line, and not less than serious injury.

For the boatheader that is not all; now he must unship the rudder and change to the huge steering oar. To do so there is a lanyard which, at a single pull, takes the pintels of the rudder from the gudgeons; the rudder is hung outboard on the port quarter by securing the lanyard to a cleat on the cuddy-board. Now during all the fighting of the whale, to meet all the sudden turns, all emergencies of maneuver, he must use the steering oar. Just sometimes, when the whale tows the boat steadily, he may be able to to take the oar inboard.

It is twenty-two feet long, this steering oar, or even twenty-three feet; in use it is supported on an iron brace on the port side of the stern post. Its blade, of course, must be vertical in the water, to have purchase for steering; to keep vertical with greater ease it has not only a shaped handle at its upper end, but a foot below that, another peglike handle standing at right angles. So used this oar is the most effective of steering agents, as I have seen, meeting emergency with great flexibility. It can also scull the boat in such narrow, tricky places as the rock-girt passage up to the slip at Salão.

The Azores whaleboat has six pulling oars (the Yankee boats had five), and they are as massive partners as you would expect for that great steering oar. Because they must strike evenly, and because the boat is shaped with an even curve from bows to stern, the oars are not all of the same length; there are two oars each of three lengths—sixteen feet, seventeen feet, eighteen feet. From bows to midships the length increases; from midships to stern it decreases. Harpooner oar is sixteen feet, bows seventeen feet, midships eighteen feet, line eighteen feet, tub seventeen feet, after sixteen feet.

The oarsmen sit one to a thwart and, to balance the ponderous length and weight of the oars, each man sits the whole thwart's width away from his oarlock. The harpooner sits on the port side to pull a starboard oar and the bow man sits to starboard to pull a port oar, and the others alternate in the same pattern. Because of the whale's acuteness of hearing, and thus the consummate need for quietness, each oar is muffled with mat at the point where it lies in the oarlock. The whale line, when ready, passes up the midships line of the boat above the oars.

So it is until the hunt comes within about a hundred yards of the whale; then even muffled oars are thought to be too noisy, too disturbing, too likely to warn the whale. Paddles, till now stowed under the gunwale, replace the oars; the men, facing forward, sit on the gunwales and paddle those last deadly yards.

That is the usual way; but sometimes it can be seen that the whale is close to sounding, and if a dart is to be made it

must be made quickly. Then there is no paddling; speed
must come before all and the boat goes on the whale with a
furious pulling of oars, so that the dart may be made before
the whale sounds. [No more than a moment may be crucial
then; so much so indeed that sometimes the boatheader will
take one hand from the steering oar and add his thrust to
the after oar, pushing with the palm as the after oarsman
pulls.]

When, going on the whale by pulling, the dart is made
and the harpoon gone home, upon that instant the boat
backs water a stroke to clear (if that may be) the awful upflung threat of the tail. Then, if all is well, the oars are
peaked, as a precaution against fouling the swingeing, kicking
run of the line. Oars boated in the usual fashion could offer
such a risk, so, within the boat opposite each oarlock, below
the gunwale, there is a hole into which the handle of the oar
is put; then they are said to be peaked, and are not a danger

but a trough in which the line can run. And indeed the oars are ready, when the whale's run spends its power, to haul slack line, and, if it is opportune, to pull up to the whale for the first thrust of the lance.

It cannot be said that the delighting beauty of Azorean whaleboats owes nothing to aesthetic impulse—no one who knows Portugal and the Portuguese can doubt the indigenous bubbling up of their sense of beauty, their finding delicious fun in beauty; but the essential character of the craft is born of their function. They are supremely practical boats for a highly specialized purpose—so specialized as to make them less fit for more general purposes. For what they have to do, for the circumstances in which they do it, they are very fine sea boats; but it must be said again that what they do is something for at least fairly fine weather. Whaling is not something which may be done in tempest or even rough weather short of that. To meet its proper purpose, the Azorean whaleboat is a delicate, almost fragile craft, unfit for the riding out of tempests.

Senhor Lucas da Silva told me of an occasion when three Pico boats were being moved from one port to another and, in that short voyage, were overtaken by one of those hurricanes that come so suddenly here. For a while, the crews fought the towering thrash of the seas, seeking to reach land, seeking by rowing to match the storm. But they were lost, all of them, the boats smashed and foundered.

Sometimes, Senhor Lucas da Silva said, a launch may be towing whaleboats, perhaps three of them, and be set upon by a storm. Then, if the storm grows too furious, the crews must come aboard the launch and the whaleboats be abandoned. Better, then, to save men rather than boats.

CHAPTER

6

THE LITTLE street under Burnt Mountain, leading
from the harbor, is narrow and quiet. It threads through with
a soft shimmer of light trapped between the flat white
façades. Children, mutely curious and staring, stand at the
doorways. It is so quiet, so placid in the little street that you
might think that all the time and event and drama of the
world had ceased to be. But in this street there is a doorway,
very wide and set deeply back within a curving-in of white
walls, that is the entrance to the whaling center of Fayal.
From here run all the nerves of the system, to the harbor,
to the whaleboat stations, to the tow boats hunting at sea.

It is dim as you go in after the sunny dazzle outside; but
soon you see that the place is long and lofty and indeed not
unlike a great cavern, dropping down from street level. In
the low light there seems first to be a confusion of things, of
maritime oddments busily crammed into every foot; then
you see that there is order, the tightly stowed order of the
whaleboats. And so it must be because here everything is

done—the boats made and repaired, the whalecraft forged, the whale lines stored and tended. Here too is the master radio that gives eyes and ears to every moment of the hunt.

Just within the door there are whaleboats that seem immensely long in this confinement, and, even here, they are immaculately stowed with all their gear as if still they must be ready to answer an instant's call to sea. There, in the bows, are the harpoons and the lances, greased and ready, heads within the protectors below the gunwale strakes; there are the oars and paddles and in the stern the boat hatchet. The line tubs are filled and neat, and masts and sails lie the boat's length. In the dim quiet, out of sound of surf and sea, there is an oddity in such exactly ordered readiness; but the rule is inviolable—there must never be the least departure

from seagoing order. This inflexibility is a shield against disaster.

Beyond the whaleboats are tow launches, tressled-up for renovation, and across the central gangway is the workshop, the line stores, all else. Here, by hand, everything is made, the harpoons, the lances, everything of the boats and in the boats. In these artifacts there is an extraordinary continuity; in the manner of their making, in the precise order of their use is a living tradition that, indigenous now, has come unchanged from the Yankee whalers. The harpoon used now in Azorean whaling has seen only the smallest change since 1848; nothing could symbolize better how astonishing a survival this open-boat whaling is.

Till 1848 the harpoon (or as the Yankees called it, the "iron") had a fixed head, arrow-shaped with two barbs, and its disadvantage lay in its tendency to "draw," to pull out. Then, in 1848, there came the toggle-headed iron, the Temple Gig, and, but for one small detail, the Azoreans use it now unchanged. Its inventor was James Temple, a Negro of New Bedford; he was a blacksmith whose trade was the making of "craft" for the whalers. There had been other experimental designs for toggle-headed irons, but none was so simply and reliably effective as his; its principle was that the head was pivoted on the shank so that, the harpoon having been darted and strain taken, the head swung out at right angles to the shank, crosswise in the tissues. In that original design the toggle head pivoted from within a channel in the shank, but in its later and final nineteenth-century form the shank lay within a channel in the head until the head swung out. So, now, the harpoon used in the Azores is exactly the same, a hand-fashioned, hand-hurled weapon—an astonishing continuation of past into present when the mechanical ingenuities of modern whaling threaten extinction to whales.

The toggle head is made from cast steel and, at its point, is needle-sharp; on one side it has a quite shallow barb and on the other it has an even crescent-shaped curve. The shank is of wrought iron, so that under stress it will bend but not break. Its end is flattened and fits within the channeled throat of the head; the two are secured by a steel pin through head and shank. So that the head shall remain against the shank until the dart is made, it is drilled again below the pivot and a wooden pin, matchstick-thick, is tightly fitted through the drilling and through a corresponding drilling through the shank, where it lies within the

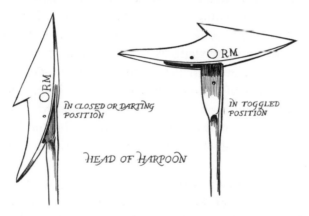

IN CLOSED OR DARTING POSITION

IN TOGGLED POSITION

HEAD OF HARPOON

channel of the head. The ends of the wood are cut off flush. When the dart has been made and the strain taken, the wooden pin snaps, and the head swings out and is toggled.

On the head, just above the steel pin, a mark is engraved —the initials of the whaling company and, sometimes, also the year of its making. Such a harpoon I have, presented to me in Horta, marked RM, showing that it belonged to Reis e Martins Lda. of Horta. There is a purpose in such marking. Throughout the history of open-boat whaling, first from New England and then in the Azores, there has been intense and often lethally dangerous rivalry between boats; it was common for more than one boat to chase and harpoon the same whale, leading to disputes of possession. The marking of harpoons helps in resolving priorities. Though the amalgamation of companies in the Azores into larger units has diminished rivalry, it still pricks into greater daring the whalers of today—I think indeed that were there no commerical competitiveness at all, the passion of their approach to whaling would still hone a fine edge of rivalry.

The length of the steel head is standardized at seven and five-eighths inches, and though the one I have is but seven inches, it may be assumed that the loss of length has come from much sharpening. "It has killed many whales," they said to me when presenting it. The whole length of the harpoon, without its shaft, is two feet nine inches, and of this one foot eleven inches is the shank of wrought iron seven-sixteenths of an inch in diameter. At its end it swells to a cone-shaped socket into which the shaped top of the shaft is fitted; the manner of that is invariable, and has come unchanged certainly from the early part of the nineteenth century.

The shaft, of local wood, is six feet long; at its butt end it is chamfered, but as it tapers upward the chamfering is lost till it becomes entirely cylindrical. The tip is pared with an adze to fit the socket of the shank—which it does so well that when shaft is fitted to socket, taps of the shaft on the ground jam the union. The join is so made because it is important that no touch of hard surface shall impair the toggle's razor edge.

Meanwhile the cone shape of the socket has been whipped down its length with marlin so that it may give a better-gripping surface for the jamming of what is called the iron-strap, and lessen the risk of the iron-strap chafing

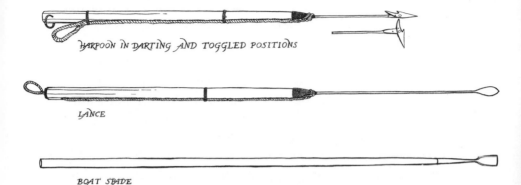

HARPOON IN DARTING AND TOGGLED POSITIONS

LANCE

BOAT SPADE

against the iron of the cone. This iron-strap is a length of rope, not much longer than the shaft and of the same rope as the whale line; its upper end is taken tightly in a round bend about the shank and secured with an eye splice (or loop). Thus, under pressure, it will jam tightly against the swell of the socket. This fastening, in the old New England term, is "the hitches," and the way of doing it has passed unaltered to the Azoreans.

Now, at its other end, up to a foot from the base of the shaft, the strap is finished with a quite large eye splice; this is "the becket." The becket's first purpose is in making the whole weapon tight and secure; a stout piece of wood is passed through it and toggled across two strong uprights— a doorway is often used. If it is a doorway, the butt of the shaft is jammed against the door step and a man draws down with all his weight on the shaft, pulling its top down at an angle to the doorway so that the strap is stretched with the utmost tautness against the shaft. Now, at two places down the shaft, the strap and shaft are whipped together by several turns of marlin. Each whipping is fixed by two copper tacks to prevent riding up, and the weapon is finished apart from a piece of light line which is passed through a hole in the butt and spliced into a loop. This formidable weapon is about eight and a half feet long and heavy.

Four harpoons so mounted are carried aboard a whale-boat, and of these, two are "live irons." A live iron is one already attached to the whale line, and the two are known as first and second irons. The first iron, that which will be used first in fastening the whale, is made fast to the box line, to the three to four fathoms of line that the harpooner holds and the further twenty-five fathoms coiled in front of him in the box. The forward end of the box line is taken first through the light-line loop at the shaft's end, then fastened to the loop of the becket by a double-becket hitch; the function of the light-line loop is to save the shaft. After the dart has been made, after the lurch of the whale's vast weight comes upon the harpoon, the whippings that hold the strap to the shaft break at once, the shaft slips from the socket, and the shaft, saved by the loop, rides freely until it may be recovered.

To the second iron is bent about four fathoms of line, the short warp, and that is attached to the whale line by a bowline, and thus may run freely. First and second irons are so arranged because it is the harpooner's purpose, if he may, to dart both, thereby more securely fastening the whale. That is the purpose, and sometimes it is achieved—the boat comes in on the whale, the first iron is darted, and immediately the harpooner will dart the second if he is given the time. But often the whale sounds upon the instant; there is no time for the second dart. Now, to leave the second iron within the boat, flying loose upon the kicking burning-out of the line, would be too great a danger; the harpooner throws it overboard to be recovered at the hunt's end.

During the chase, until the crisis of harpooning, the two live irons lean in readiness against the thigh board to the right of the harpooner, with the first iron nearer to him. The other two irons of the four lie across the thwarts on the port side, covered by a piece of canvas—and even in this, precise tradition is observed. So they have always been stowed, so they always must. There is no detail of stowage or procedure not strictly governed by custom; a rigid precision of traditional order makes subconscious habit, so that in the sharp seconds of greatest danger there shall be no calamity of cross-purposes.

When the whale has had its first runs, when it has sounded, run again, when it has begun to tire, the boat must haul up on it to kill it; the means for that is the lance. A whaleboat carries two or three lances. The head of the lance is cast steel, leaf-shaped, needle-pointed, razor-sharp all around. Below the head is the shank, wrought iron but not short as is that of the harpoon, four and one-half to five feet long and ending in a cone-shaped socket for fitting on the shaft. The shaft is the same as that for the harpoon (but with a copper ferrule), and is mounted similarly—the marlin whipping of the cone is the same, and the lance-strap has the same looped attachment over it. The strap, though, is lighter, and there is only one whipping of strap and shaft, halfway down the shaft. Four inches from the butt, the strap is taken through a slot in the shaft and from there out through a hole in the center of the butt's face. There a loop is spliced, fitting snugly against the face of the butt. So mounted, all the lance's length is clean and easy and unencumbered; there is nothing to trip or snarl the harpooner's hands at the crucial moment.

To the lance is attached the lance warp, eight fathoms of light line bent onto the loop of the lance strap and secured at its other end to the clumsy cleat. This is so the lance can be recovered after a thrust—and the lance may be used several or even many times before the whale is killed. During the chase the lances are stowed well forward, across the thwarts on the starboard side, close to the harpooner.

It is important that at no time shall the keen edges and bright faces of harpoon and lance heads be exposed to the least risk of damage; the manner of securing that is a direct inheritance from New England whaling. When out of use in the boat, the heads are enclosed in sheaths made from flats of hardwood which close on each other on a leather hinge. The inside surfaces are hollowed out to hold the heads, and, at the end away from the hinge, are tied around the shank by marlin.

The lance is still the only means for the killing of the whale, and it is one of the more extraordinary factors in the whole extraordinary relic that is Azorean whaling that it should still be used. This is so primitive and deadly dangerous a way, and there is so much apparent advantage in the use of such other means as firearms. By the latter part of the nineteenth century the New England whalers had begun to use such aids, and among them a form of bomb lance. The Azoreans did indeed take over certain firearms with the rest of the New England inheritance, but forsook them at a very early stage; it was a corollary to this that in the last years of Yankee whaling, when the whaleships were largely manned by Portuguese, and they mainly Azoreans, there was a return to hand weapons. Whatever may have been the reason, it is pertinent that, except for old, solitary bulls, sperm whales consort in schools. Explosions frighten and disperse them.

There has been experimentation with bomb lances in the Azores more recently, and I was told of it by Senhor Tomas Alberto de Azevedo, who tried them—but I should first say

something of him. He, alone, could stand as a symbol of
Azorean whaling.

He could do so because in him the inner fundamental
that, as I became convinced, is the spur to this searingly
dangerous and strikingly unprofitable pursuit is more than
normally obvious. The typical Azorean whaleman wears over
the inner burn an amiable urbanity; he is gentle in his ways.
But in Senhor Tomas Alberto the flicker of the flame is
visible. As he talks of whaling, eye and voice ignite, though it
is long since he retired from it to run the company that owns
Espirito Santo and her little sister ships. But he was a whaler
and he came of whalers. An uncle, Antonio Vicira, lost a
leg in the old whaling days (Tomas Alberto owns his house
now), and another uncle, Manuel Victoriano, died whaling
off Flores. He disappeared over the bows and was never seen
again. Senhor Tomas Alberto was a whaler for eighteen
years, and now, in safe retirement, the burn of it disturbs
him still.

He experimented first, he told me, with a simple bomb
lance that exploded upon the thrust being made, and to
that extent its behavior was exemplary. But unfortunately
not only the whale took the brunt; the explosion threw
those in the boat head over heels. Undefeated, though
shaken, he devised a means to make the explosion safe by
remoteness. He made an explosive head to fit over the lance
head, with eighty-two feet of insulated wire to reach back to
the boat so that, from that immunity of distance, the bomb
could be electrically detonated. This seemed at first to be
successful, a means of avoiding many long dangerous hours
that are often a part of killing by unarmored lances. But
there came a time when a whale turned at the crucial
moment and came down upon the launch that fired the

lance, so that the explosion came close against her. "We abandoned explosive lances," Tomas Alberto said.

Upon the darting of the harpoon, the first line to go is the three or four fathoms held by the harpooner and the twenty-five fathoms coiled in the box. The old custom was to throw it overboard, to give that brief cushion of time to allow the boat to backwater. This front line is lighter than the tub line, though it was, in the past, of the same kind. The New Englanders used manila, but the Azoreans changed to hemp and then to sisal for the tub line. But for the box line the modern world has made a contribution.

It was during the last war, Senhor Tomas Alberto told me, that a German ship was in Horta, and he was impressed by a thick rope of nylon aboard her. He begged a piece and unraveled it to make an eighty-two foot length of the right thickness for box line; he found it altogether better, lighter, easier to handle in the demanding moments of harpooning. But for the tub line, sisal is used still. Nylon is too slippery, without enough friction, and as a running line it burns hands because its lack of purchase demands so much grip.

The box line's circumference is one and a half inches, but that of the tub line is two inches, and of that there are 120 fathoms in each tub, a total of 240 fathoms. The coiling down of the line in the tubs is something for exacting care; the fouling of one coil could bring disaster, loss of life perhaps, or it could cause the loss of the whale. The line must slip away easily, coil by coil, and, need it be said, there is an exact and tradition-honored way of doing it. The coiling down is by what is called Flemish flakes. First the end of the line is brought up the inside of the tub, over the edge, and there given an eye splice. Then the first flake is begun by coiling from the outside, and so on till the coils reach the center. Then the line is brought back to the outside of the circumference and another flake laid from outside to center, and thus it goes till the tub is full. When the boat is not hunting, the tubs are covered with canvas made waterproof by painting; when the boats cast off from the tow launches, when the chase begins, the line in the waist tub is bent to that in the after tub, the latter being the one from which the line goes first, going from there around the loggerhead. That, the turns around the loggerhead, is the only means used to check the line against the running of the whale; in no other way is the line fast to the boat. To make fast to the boat could mean that a whale that ran fast, and took all the line suddenly, could capsize and perhaps drag under the boat before the line could be cut.

If it is apparent that a whale is going to take all the line and there is time enough, one of the tow launches will come up with a spare line which can be bent onto the eye splice over the edge of the waist tub.

At times the line must be cut, times of dire emergency. If the boat is stove, if the line has gone foul and might swamp the boat, if a man has fouled the line, or any of those malignant events that may come so easily to a whaleboat, then the line must be cut. In the bows, beside the harpooner on the port side, the boat hatchet is stowed just aft of the thigh board, under the gunwale; and on the thigh board itself is nailed the sheath of the forward boat knife. An after-boat knife is nailed to the cuddyboard. But, invariably, it is the boat hatchet which must be used to cut line—when the line is singing out to the wild run of a whale, it would turn a knife's blade.

Aboard a whaleboat there is also a boat spade, which is a smaller relation of the cutting spades used in the working up of a whale on the flensing platform. This boat spade has a head of cast steel eight or nine inches long and three or

three and a half inches wide. It goes by a short shank to its
iron socket, to which the nine feet of shaft is fitted. The
boat spade has its use when a whale has been killed and must
be prepared for towing. The boat is hauled up alongside the
whale, and a hole is cut with the boat spade through which
the towing strap can be reeved. The buoyant skittish movement of the boat, on the lift and roll of the sea, makes it a
precarious task, one for strength and steadiness. It is easier
to chop the hole in the relatively accessible fluke than anywhere, and although it is often done so, the whale tows at
something of an angle, making more resistance to the
launch's pull. So, if it may be done, the hole is made in the
head, giving a straight draw. This is advantageous when a
school of whales has been found and several killed; then
several may be towed in line astern. For the reeving of the
towing strap, a grapnel and a boat hook, part of the whaleboat's equipment too, are used. The strap may be wire rope,
a short warp doubled, or, as I have seen it, a short chain
carried on the tow launch.

The whaleboats also carry waifs, flags for signaling, one
red, one white, one blue; they do so by the regulations of the
Grémio dos Armadores da Pesca da Baleia, the guild of
whaling owners. The red waif is a signal for help—there may
be an emergency, a man injured, a boat damaged, or it may
be a call for the service of the launch, such as for more line.
The white waif is used as a signal between boats of different
companies, a signal to share a whale—but that is something
only done in an emergency because the companies are
stringently competitive. However, if a boat has fastened a
whale and then suffered an accident, such as being stove in,
though technically it still has the ownership of the whale it
is in no practical position to take the whale. If then it
signals with its white waif to the boat of another company,

the two together may save the whale and then go halves on
it. The blue waif is a recognition signal—between two boats
that they are of the same company, or to the cliff lookouts
that those two or more are hunting together.

Waifs have another use, that of marking killed whales.
Occasionally a whale may sink (unless it can be kept afloat
by lines from whaleboats or launch); but normally a whale
will float, though very inconspicuously. In all the shift and
glint of the sea, on even a calm day it becomes hard to see
at even quite a short distance in spite of the rigid and
characteristic upthrust of its flipper. The greater bulk is submerged, leaving just a small island of flank awash in the
surface—and, unless the day is far gone or the whale was a
solitary one, the hunt goes on; the killed whale must be
collected at the day's end. So, for its easier finding, it is
marked with a waif. The staff of the waif must be secure

in the slit cut for it, so at its end there are from one to three notches made, like the barb of a fish hook, with the barb facing up the staff. This catches in the fibrous texture of the blubber and holds firmly.

The rules of the Grémio dos Armadores da Pesca da Baleia also decree a rather starkly basic provision for survival at sea—which has so often been proved a need. There must be aboard each boat a keg of water and some ship's biscuit, a lamp, and a compass. The keg is of wood, cooper-made and cylindrical in section but tapering inward from base to top, and with a wooden lid. The lamp, the biscuit, and the water are stowed within the cuddy, the space under the cuddy-board; the compass goes in one of the two drawers on the underside of the cuddy-board. The other one holds canvas and copper tacks for emergency repair if the boat is stove by a whale. Customarily, boat crews carry whistles so that, if they are overtaken by night and are in difficulty, they may be located by launches.

Two other standard pieces of boat equipment are the piggin and boat bucket, both of wood and cooper-made, the bucket with a rope handle and the piggin with one of its staves continuing above the top of the vessel to form a handle. The specified purpose of the piggin is for bailing, but both it and the boat bucket are used for "wetting line." The two after oarsmen, with bucket and piggin, tip water upon the line as, flake by flake, it leaves the tubs. Were this not done, and were the line not wetted at the loggerhead too, it would catch fire, so great is the friction there. Even so, the line smokes at the loggerhead.

All the boats' equipment, every item, has its daily inspection; it is checked, tended, kept to the instant's readiness. And, constantly, repair, replacement, repainting, every sort of servicing, continues in the cavernous premises under

Burnt Mountain. There is no part of the apparatus (apart from radiotelephones) that is not made or serviced there—the rope for lines is not, of course, made there, but all its deployment to any use is. In the forge the "craft" is made, harpoons, lances, and boat spades, and the launches and *canoas* are built in the other part of the building. In the low-lighted quiet of that place is the pulse of all the salt and sting and wild danger of the hunt upon the sea around.

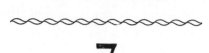
*T*HE ALARM may come at any time and send the shivering thrill of expectancy prickling from stomach to head. But more than any other time it comes in the still time of even low light between dawn and sunrise, at six o'clock and not long after, at the time of the year of greatest whalers' chance. One or more of the lonely lookouts at their aeries will see a whale—raise a blow—and the rocket is fired to signal the boats' crews. And, at that same time (as it is on Fayal anyway), radiotelephone will alert the launches in the harbor at Horta and the whaling center in its quiet street. There, too, the rocket fires, so that it may signal the moment to the launches' crews. At the firing, the men come running, shouting as they come; their cry is always the same, the same electrifying cry that has been the beginning of such unnumbered dangerous days. *"Baleia! Baleia!"* they shout.

Within minutes the launches throb into life, churn with a fury of urgency across and out of the harbor, beat around the coast toward the boat station nearest the sighting of the whale. The engineman is in command, there is a man at the wheel, and often another man or more aboard. The launch is rakish, lean-lined, about forty feet long, and now, racing to action, her engine drives her at eighteen knots. Aft, in the well of the launch, there are two drums of gas, two spare tubs of whale line, a keg of water, wire straps, and light chains for whale towing straps. Forward, on the deck before the wheelhouse, there are harpoons and lances fastened down, heads in sheaths, a boat hook, and a boat spade.

When the whaleboat station is reached, at Salão or at Varadouro, the whaleboats will be waiting, already launched, tittuping on the swell until the launch edges up to them to take their tow warps. Then the tow warps are toggled under the clumsy cleat, the launches open throttle, and, two or three to a launch, the whaleboats are towed headlong to the vicinity of the whale's blow. That may be three or four miles or thirty miles, and as they go, in a white foam of wake, the whaleboats' crews huddle aft to lighten the bows so that the seas may not swamp in.

So they go, engines roaring, whaleboats bouncing, skimming and sidling, and every quarter of an hour or so, enginemen on their radiotelephones talk to the high-perched lookouts, checking their bearings, checking the number of blows raised. When, as the lookouts tell them, they are near the whales, near to sighting, a lookout may be raised in a bosun's chair to the masthead to scan till he sees the low plumy blow. Then he sees it, small and distant, and perhaps sees several, and at a mile's distance the launches stop, cut their engines. Now there must be quiet, no sound to alarm the whales. The whaleboats cast off, the covers are taken from the line tubs, and the harpooner bends waist-tub line to after-tub line, then bends on the live irons. If there is a fair wind the mast is stepped and sail hoist and the boatheader, aft on the standing cleats, steers by the tiller. If there is no wind (or not enough), the oars are manned, the long oars muffled in their oarlocks so that they shall make no betraying sound. The boatheader, high on his cleats, searches ahead, steers by the great steering oar; he whispers his orders and there is silence in the boat. A school of whales that is frightened may "gallie"—divide and scatter.

A school that remains close, does not gallie, allows a concentration of the hunt; a scattered school may mean many hours of frustrating, unpatterned chasing, and so easily, too easily, that may happen. So it is typically; but it may sometimes be that a whale will show a queer indifference, will loiter at the surface for its quick undoing. Such a whale is easily fastened.

But that is not characteristic. The men bend to their oars, pulling hard, and luck is sometimes so much with them that the chase is short—the whale continues at the surface, the approach is made and finished and the dart made all within not much more than minutes, a quarter of an hour perhaps. Much more often every deviousness of chance comes between the chase's start and end. The whale is so sensitively attuned, there is such an immensity of sea; the whale may seem settled at the surface, "having his spoutings out"—blowing and blowing as the boat comes up—then, as the harpooner braces himself and takes his iron the whale rounds out, peaks his flukes, and sounds. How then is it to be found again? How, in so much sea, is even that great creature to be pinpointed again to practical proximity?

All is not as amorphous as it seems, though; there *is* pattern—there is pattern and there is that which seems extrasensory, instinctive, but which is presumably a racial accumulation of experience. The whalers, as I have seen, appear to *feel* the whale—they will be relaxed and unexpectant or, for no apparent reason, tense and hanging on the moment. Certain factors they know; a whale, they will tell you, goes usually with the sun, from east to west, and if there is no complete infallibility in that, it is rare that a whale will go against the sun. And, when a whale rounds out, then sounds, its tail, the great horizontal flukes, will rear above the surface and the angle of them is an indication (to eyes trained to know) as to where it will reappear. Yet when that has been allowed, there appears to be something akin to supranormality in the way whalers can continue contact with a sounding whale.

A sounding may be short or long, five minutes or half an hour, and exceptionally it may be longer; the reappearance may be anywhere in the formless roll of sea, and it may be as much as a mile away. But with their queer perceptiveness the whalers will mostly anticipate it; though they may drift, relaxed, during the sounding, they will usually have eyes trained in the direction of the reemergence—though indeed, if that is at all close, the sound of the whale's first blow is revealing enough, and this is followed by a series of blows. It is now, as the whale has his spoutings out, that is the best moment for fastening; the men pull hard to close on the whale, to dart the harpoon before it shall sound again. Even then, when they are almost upon the whale, when the harpooner is up and braced against the thigh board with harpoon ready, it may sound again. There may be as much patient attrition as intrepidity in whaling.

But the time will come, the ripeness of moment, for "going on the whale," and then for the last hundred yards there will be an intense and brittle urgency in the boat. Depending on the situation, the men use oars or paddles with feverish urgency while the boatheader exhorts them on in whispers—"*Força, força!*" he says. If they are under sail, so they will go in, with paddles too. For this last hundred yards of the chase the direction of it is precise, not as chance may be.

The approach is related to the nature of the sperm whale's vision, and the boatheader must decide which of two usual approaches is more practical. The better part of the whale's sight is to the side, on its beam; it is sharply limited behind and at least partially limited in front—though the longitudinal grooves running from the eyes forward along the head probably give some forward vision if the whale is "head-out."

The boatheader may decide to go in *cabeça com cabeça,* head and head as it is in English,[1] but he will prefer to go on the flukes; thus it is far more often done. Going head and head, the boat is directed toward the great sheer of the whale's forehead, going into that narrow zone between the arcs of vision, keeping the hump barely to the left of the spout until near enough to sight on the recurrent showing of the forehead itself. Then the boat is very near; the harpooner stands up, against the clumsy cleat, thigh braced in the notch; he holds the harpoon poised to dart. The boatheader turns the boat out of the narrow approach, to the side; at the precise moment, he throws his weight on the steering oar, "lays the boat on." The bows turns in just behind the head and, at that exact moment, the harpooner makes his dart. The whale is fastened; the crew goes astern a couple of strokes, the whale sounds or runs, the line pours away.

But going head and head is dangerous, more dangerous than the inescapable accepted danger; and only the smallest misjudgment, a momentarily premature darting of the har-

---

[1] *Literally, "head with head."*

poon, may lodge it too far forward, in the head. The tissue is tough there, too resistant for secure fastening. There is, however, one advantage—because the boat and whale are moving one toward the other there is the better chance of quick overtaking.

Going on the flukes has more advantages and at least a little less danger. The normal nature of the pursuit tends to put boat and whale in such relative positions that it is the more natural approach, and there is a wider zone outside the whale's arc of vision. So, for that last hundred yards, the boat comes in from behind the whale, keeping hump and spout in line until, for the final yards, the boat turns to come up on the whale's quarter. Then, going at the hump, the boat is laid on; the harpooner, braced and ready, darts the harpoon, the boat backs water two strokes.

The final proximity of boat to whale, at the moment of darting, is variable; in the commonest practice the dart is made from a little off, from one to three fathoms off most usually, but it may be more, four fathoms. A very strong harpooner may even dart more than that—and the long dart has the critical advantage that it lessens the whalers' greatest danger, that of the awful upflinging of the whale's great tail as it sounds. Its disadvantage is that there is less certainty of a very secure fastening; it is for the chance of that that a boat will sometimes go on a whale "wood to blackskin."

Then the bows are actually run against the whale's flank, and the harpooner, who has been waiting with harpoon above his head, plunges it down, throwing all his weight, almost throwing himself over the whale. The dart so made goes deep, up to the socket, through the blubber, into the muscle—doing indeed with maximum thoroughness what must always be done for secure fastening. The harpoon which is not "fleshed" is likely to draw; the head cannot toggle against the blubber's underside. If he is able, a harpooner will always make his dart forward, in the thorax in preference to farther aft, for the chance of the head toggling under the ribs. Wherever it is made, he will if he can dart his second live iron immediately. The hand harpoon, formidable weapon as it is, is a puny thing to see against so great a beast.

So far description has been of the whale and the boat, one boat, as if they, just those two, shared a lonely sea; invariably it is otherwise. Nearly always there are other boats of the same company, and quite often boats of a rival company, or, as it is now, of a rival association of companies. Between the boats the sting of rivalry is sharp, a spur to desperate racing for first fastening of the whale; so it is

anyway if the whale is solitary. If there is a school of whales, each boat may have its own business. Formerly, before amalgamations of companies, when the boats of several might be involved in the chase of one whale, their rivalry had a scorching fury of recklessness; two (or more) boats would go simultaneously hell-bent upon the whale, chancing collision, chancing multiple entanglement of boats and whale. It has even occurred that, as one boat was about to close on the whale, another swept in, between whale and first boat, whereupon the first harpooner hurled his harpoon over the rival and, incredibly, fastened the whale. It is as incredible that no awful and fatal entanglement followed, and record says nothing of that.

The extent of commercial competitiveness has been reduced since then by amalgamations; but it does not appear that this has really lessened the nag of rivalry in practice. The economic urge to such fires of competition is plain enough—the successful company has the whale, its crew has its share of the value, and the rule is inviolable that ownership of the whale goes to the first boat to fasten. But you must look beyond that, at the nature of the men, to understand fully why rivalry's flame licks so hotly.

There is a clue in something told to me by Senhor Tomas Alberto. In the old days, he said, those old days of furious rivalry, lookout men had private codes of signals with whalemen. By all sorts of little devices they would give privy directions for the quicker locating of a whale—a hat on or a hat off, a pullover pulled up, such things. Then he hastened to add that the motive was not a commercial one; it was a sporting one—and, looking at Senhor Tomas Alberto, the truth of that could not be doubted. His was the emotional attitude of a hunter of big game; he had been paid, but the hunt was the thing. Incidentally, he told me that once he had taken out a big-game hunter on a foray after whales, and brought that hunter to an acute state of worry and alarm by how close they went to the whale. The hunter came back content to have a future confined to his big game; it was so much safer, he said.

Sporting is the word you may use for the hot fever of the chase, and if that breeds fierce rivalry it also brings a strong comradeship which, if expedient, is also of the blood and spirit. Whalemen are quick and ready to help each other, man for man, boat for boat. In any case, merely to be practical, boats commonly work as a team. If whales are few, several boats of one company may fasten the same whale to kill it more quickly, in spite of the probability of difficulty in the handling of the boats.

Because the system of the hunt is so orderly, so much to a method, a formula, and because at the time of crisis all is so orderly and without panic, it might be supposed that these are men without fear, men with nothing but the fierce ecstasy of the chase. But to such men fear is that which sharpens, puts a fine point to readiness. At the moment of crescendo toward finality the sharp-tremored pulse of fear can be felt through the boat. It is told of one whaleboat skipper whom I know that at the going-in on a whale he is in so acute a state of nervous tension that not a word he says can be understood. Yet he is a skipper of noted intrepidity and consistent success.

When the harpoons have been darted, the whale fastened, great as has been the hazard of that, the most perilous part of the hunt has to come. The whale must be killed, and the time for that may be short or long. José Rufino, a boatheader and veteran of many kills, told me that he has known whales to die in two minutes from a lucky lancing that has found a major artery; but, as often, there have been twelve hours to the death. Luck may vary, skill may vary, but whales are no less variable; and the strongest, most enduring whale may not be the biggest.

When the harpoon goes home, at that first pang, the whale's response is immediate and explosive. It may go in a hurricane rush on or close to the surface, but more usually it will sound, and then the huge upflinging of its flukes may catch the boat, shattering its frail timbers. But, there being no accident, the whale sounds and the line pours away. By bucket and piggin,water is thrown upon the line as the flakes tumble from the tubs so that it may not take fire.

Then the whale's sounding levels off, and, sooner or later, the first awful impetus slackens; it is time to take tentative turns of line at the loggerhead. If the whale has tired enough the boat may tow, leaping forward; more often, at that jab of pressure, the whale will sound again, pulling down the bows so that the boat takes water. The line is loosed from the loggerhead and surges out again. But there comes a time when the whale's first wild brunt of energy is expended; it begins to lift in the water, slacken so consistently that line may be gained. The men are standing now, astride the thwarts, hauling on the line, taking it down the midships line to the boatheader, who coils it down on his platform— coils it down with such exacting neatness and care that coil will not foul coil when, soon, the whale runs again. Run it does, and the line gained burns away.

Even the wildest whale will wear down, and the time comes when its runs slacken and the boatheader can make his turns at the loggerhead and keep them. Now the boat tows, it tears away in the whale's wake; this is the "Nantucket sleigh ride." The boat's headlong ride is fast; Senhor Tomas Alberto estimated it for me at ten or twelve knots, but I think he must have meant that as an average—the pace is variable. The more frantic gouts of speed can come nearer to twenty knots or even, perhaps, more. The pace is variable and the towing is intermittent. Repeatedly the boat-header will have to free his turns from the loggerhead, then snub them again, and at intervals there may even be the chance to haul slack line.

But a whale may be too furious for such cat's play; it may become apparent that the frenzy of its runs is going to take all the line. Then a launch must be called. It comes alongside, an empty tub is passed to it, and it gives in return a full tub, the line of which is bent to the fast-melting remnant of the original line. Or, perhaps because a launch is not near enough, a "loose boat" (one that has not fastened) is called. To the harpooner of the fast boat it gives the end of its line, and he, by a rolling hitch, makes it fast to his own line just outboard of the chocks. Now the first boat, the former fast boat, is loose; the second boat is now a fast boat—and all this interchange must be done in the moment-to-moment unpredictability of the whale, when a pause in the run may become instantly another fury of running and the line heating close to combustion. When the line runs it becomes too hot for hand touch; an oarlock is used. And, when all has been done, it may sometimes be that the whale is lost, its fury outlasting all maneuvers. While I was in Horta, a whale fastened not far off Castelo Branco took three lines and then was lost, it and those 720 fathoms of line.

That, though, is exceptional; more often than otherwise the boat that first fastens the whale will kill it. The time comes when the power of the whale has drained enough for approach to be made for lancing; the period for that is widely variable, a few minutes occasionally, often an hour or more, and the shorter time is no suggestion that the interval to the kill will be comparably brief. Short or long it brings a tenser time of danger than did the fastening, a chilled bracing to the second's crisis; the men are bound in the common cold fire of their purpose.

Astride the thwarts they haul up on the whale, haul to crack of muscle, till, when they are near, and if the whale is quiet, they put out oars to pull, sometimes right in, "wood and blackskin." But the whale may still have strength to spare; it may be tired but beyond the power of their pulling. Then they bring the line to the bow cleats, veer obliquely on it, and come alongside for the lance's first thrust. Thus the boat is "bowed on," and that for all its deadly convenience is superlatively dangerous. There they have all the perils of proximity that they may have; they are against the vast beast, between its jaws and its flukes and too close to its flippers.

Now is the poignant time of testing for the harpooner, the time of fearful responsibility; his strength and his skill may bear almost the whole burden of the crew's survival. For the strain that lancing makes he must have very powerful legs; his skill must seek to find the "life," that place within the thorax where the thrust may be most nearly vital. If the boat has gone in wood and blackskin, if he, braced against the thigh board, is right over the whale, his whole weight and thrust and being will go into an orgasmic downward plunge of the lance. His plunging thrust will send the four or five feet of head and shank up to the socket. Then, even then, in the danger of that moment, if the whale does not immediately peak its flukes and sound, the harpooner will continue his hold and plunge the lance up and down, "churn" it as it is said. So he does it for that frightened moment, then the boat has backed water, two or so frantic strokes, up have gone the mighty flukes, the whale has sounded and the line is throbbing away. All the towing, all the hauling, must come again until there shall be another chance to lance.

The approach for lancing, wood and blackskin, has as reward for its danger the greatest effectiveness, the greatest chance of a vital thrust, but many approaches are less lethally close. Many are up to that two or three fathoms of distance that are typical of harpooning, and then the lance is hurled in the same tossing fashion; such lancings are effective enough—the eleven or twelve feet of lance is heavy, the head keen.

Whichever the way of it, the whale sounds and the lance, on its warp, is jerked free by the plunge, brought inboard again. Often the wrought-iron shank is bent and is straightened across the gunwale or, sometimes, the harpooner's knee; it must be ready for the next lancing.

There may be several more; occasionally there are many more and the grisly attritional struggle will take a bloody course of many hours. In the old days, before the advent of motor tow launches, there was no help for such protractions; now, often, a launch intervenes—as it may do if, for example, it is advantageous to kill quickly because there are many whales. The launch has its lances too, longer than those of the whaleboats because the freeboard is greater. It comes upon the whale from behind, sweeping up and in upon the whale, coming often to within three or four feet of it. The lance is driven in, the launch goes past the head, veers off sharply, and the lance, which has its warp fast to a loggerhead, is pulled out—and always it comes out with shank bent. The launch sweeps on in a wide circle and, as it goes, the lance is straightened on a special block for that purpose. Then the launch comes in again, lances again, and so continues until the death.

The death may come in moments, one vast pathetic convulsion; more often it is longer, several minutes. Then it is "the flurry," a last slow huge labor of dying for the great poor beast, a time of acute last danger for the men. The declaration of its coming is that which the old New Englanders called the "red flag," a plume of bloody spray from the spout; when that has shown, the dying monster lurches at the surface. There, moving more or less in a slow-motion circle, its life goes in a series of convulsions, of blind unpredictable slow thrashings from which the boats must stand off. Then it is over; the whale is dead, awash in the surface, flipper stiffly erect—"fin-out" as the New Englanders called it.

That then is the process for the hunting and killing of a whale, from dart to death; that is the formula. But the perils that punctuate it are too constant for there not to be many and sometimes tragic variations. The time of most acute danger is at the lancing, but the hazard of harpooning is less only by that standard. There is indeed no moment which does not demand an exactitude of care and an ordering of movement evolved from experience. The story of Francisco Machado, told to me in Horta, is an apt illustration.

Francisco Machado was a harpooner, young, only in his early twenties, and the less experienced for that. On August 15, 1948, he, in a *canoa* skippered by Manuel Barreto, put to sea from Lages do Pico. The day went well and soon they came on their whale. Now Francisco was regarded as a very promising harpooner; the spirit of those aboard was with him. The tension in the boat, the high anticipation, was greater even than is usual. Francisco made his dart and made it well; the harpoon entered deeply. But so great was the tense excitement, so high Francisco's elation, that his care slackened; he forgot to watch his feet. A turn of the leaping line took his ankle and, though upon the instant a man took the boat hatchet and cut the line, it was too late. Francisco was whisked away by the sounding of the whale. He was never seen again.

It was Senhor Tomas Alberto who told me a story to illustrate that when all seems done, when the lancing is over and the whale is dying in the "flurry," there may still be deadly danger. On October 29, 1941, the lookouts raised blows about the time of daybreak, the rockets were fired, and a number of boats with accompanying launches put to sea. Among them was the boat *Ruth*; M. Cardosa was her skipper, and the others aboard were Antonio de Carolina, José de Carolina, his brother, Gabriel Adreste, José da Praia, Antonio Mestrejão, and Antonio Casimiro. Cardosa, the skipper, and Casimiro were (as may often be the case) elderly men.

The day was a good one, with many whales, and in the afternoon *Ruth* had harpooned a whale and was standing by for the flurry; all, it seemed, was well. The attendant launch decided to give help to other boats that were struggling with whales. *Ruth* was left with her dying whale. But it, about the time of sunset, suddenly found a brief resurgence; rushed at the boat, threw it into the air, smashed it. The men were in the water, clinging to the upturned wreckage, and, ordinarily, they would have been rescued by the launch. But it and the other *canoas* were preoccupied, the accident was unnoticed; darkness fell.

Now, alone in the heaving dark and the creeping night cold—this was late October—theirs was a miserably desperate situation. The younger men pushed the two elderly men, Antonio Casimiro and M. Cardosa, onto the top of the upturned boat, onto the keel; they, according to the accustomed way, clung around the sides of the boat. Thus they waited, hoping to be found by a launch. And indeed two launches were searching, beating up and down. Senhor Tomas Alberto was aboard one of them and, he said, often they were close to the benighted boat, though they did not know it. If only, he said, they had zigzagged; unhappily they did not think of it. Meanwhile, to sharpen the forlorn torment of *Ruth's* crew,

they could see the lights of the launches but had no means to direct them—they had not, it seems, followed the common custom of having whistles.

The night dragged on, endless minutes growing to endless

hours until Antonio Casimiro knew that his end was near. Calmly he said to the others, "Goodbye." Cardosa answered him. "Yes," he said, "I know you're going. I shall join you soon." Then Antonio Casimiro slipped from the keel, into the sea. He was not seen again. A little later Cardosa slipped into the sea and was seen no more.

For the remaining five, the limping hours wore on as they, with numbed hands, clung about the boat, strength and spirit ebbing from them. Oddly it was the youngest member of the crew, the harpooner, who inspired them to survival—as they would have succumbed, drifted into numbed surrender, he strengthened them, blew into a little glow their dying ember of persistence. And so, at last, the night passed; the dawn came and in its first light they were seen by a shore lookout which directed a launch to them. They were saved, saved but at the last extremity.

The record of such grim events is long enough, but far more often than not they are accidents of inadvertence; they come not from deliberate aggressive intent by the whale, but by the chance of its monstrous thrashing. But from time to time it is otherwise; the vast beast, made furious by its torment, turns on the boats. Such a case was that of the Canecas.

There were three of them of that name, a father, his son, and another not related, and on the day of this event each in a different boat was a harpooner. It was the father's boat that went on the whale first, and he darted his harpoon, fastened successfully. Upon that moment the whale (and this was a great creature) turned in fury on the boat and bit off its bows. Now the son came in, darted his iron and fastened, but upon him too the whale came in its enormous rage, with its gaping jaws, and bit the boat. The third boat, that of the other Caneca, took the line from the second boat, but it too fell under the whale's onslaught. The whale turned on it, crunched the frail timbers.

Close by there were four other *canoas*, but they stood off; they would have nothing to do with this frenzied monster that was so clearly ready to shatter any boat that came near it. And now night was falling.

In the flotilla there were two launches, and upon them now fell the responsibility. Each in its turn put on its searchlight while the other came in with the lance, and so, turn and turn about, they fought the whale till, at eleven o'clock, it was over. The great angry ferocious creature was dead. At the factory subsequently it realized 2,375 gallons of oil. That was a huge whale, but I heard of a greater one, one brought in to Cais do Pico; it yielded seventy-three drums of fifty-three gallons each.

Not all accidents have fatal endings—nor indeed do they all bring serious injury; there are men on Fayal who can tell you of the sequence of accidents that have punctuated their years of whaling, and not one of them dire in its consequences. There was Heliodono Vardosa, now a peaceful worker of wood in Horta; for thirty years he was at sea after whales, from age sixteen to forty-six, and five or six times he was in smashed boats. A whale once came under his boat, threw it into the air; all the crew were thrown out. But, as the tale came to me, none was seriously the worse for it. And, Senhor Tomas Alberto told me, there was a whale that came under a launch, lifting it completely out of the water; the whale passed on, the launch settled sweetly back in the water.

There are, as could be expected, many oddities of chance, though often with that rather grim undertone which seems inseparable from this whaling. In 1952, they told me, a large school of whales was sighted off Capelo, and the boats swarmed out, from Fayal and from Pico, sixteen *canoas* in all. All fastened whales, and one of them, *Maria Virginia*, harpooned a cow; it, before their startled eyes, gave birth to young, forty to fifty of them. In the excitement, the jostling and peering, one man, Tomas Serafim, fell overboard. For half an hour he was swimming among the throng of baby whales; when he was picked up, his only injury was some bruising and a broken shin—and that, by Azorean whaling standards, is the most minor of injuries. This was the story told to me, and I cannot explain the eccentricity of its natural history. The truthful intentions of the story cannot be doubted, but how is it to be reconciled with the fact that the sperm whale normally has single births, with twins exceptionally? My feeling is that constant retelling of the story may have multiplied the baby whales; perhaps it is a fact that numbers of young swim with a school of adults.

The coming of radiotelephone has greatly simplified the chasing of whales; previous communications were entirely by visual means. On the raising of a blow, or a number of blows, the lookouts fired their rockets and hoisted a white flag—the latter being not for the warning of the boats' crews, but to alert other lookouts and such whalemen's families as lived in from the coast. On the killing of a whale, the flag was brought to half-mast so that the try works (those shore stations for the cutting-in of whales that preceded whale factories) might be made ready, and so that whalemen's families could prepare food against the men's return.

To give a bearing to the boats, the lookout spread two sheets so that, by keeping them in line, the bearing was maintained. If, nevertheless, the boats strayed from their right course, the lookout would make a smoke and, if the true bearing was to port, a sheet would be spread to port of the smoke. Then perhaps the boat, with no more aid, would recover the right bearing, and sheet and smoke would be taken off. When the whale sounded before the boats were in sighting distance, the lookout would make a smoke, then another to the side, port or starboard, sometimes up to four, till the boats, so directed, were going straight on the whale. Then all would be taken off. Once a skipper had sight of the peaking flukes of the whale as it sounded, no more shore directions were given; from then on he had no need of them.

Accumulation of experience, a tradition of long building, has established a code of working toward minimizing the danger of the hunt; but men may vary, the passion of the chase may burn fiercely. So Authority lays down its enforced code, a stringent system of rules for whaling. The code given here is that issued from the office of the Captain of the Port of Horta, December 1965. It leaves little room for transgression.

1. It is strictly forbidden to fish for whales with less than two vessels, one of which must be mechanically propelled. A violation of this rule will be punishable by a fine of between Esc. 500.00 to 2,000.00 [$17.75-$71.00].

2. Whalers are forbidden to spear or kill a whale if the second vessel is not near enough to come to their assistance in case of an accident. The master of the vessel who orders the spearing or killing of a whale when not within easy approach of the second vessel is liable to a fine of between Esc. 50.00 to 500.00 [$1.77-$17.75] and a prison sentence of between one and ten days.

3. If during fishing operations a member of the crew should fall overboard, the skipper or master of the vessel in question should abandon all other operations, even cut the line if necessary, and devote all his attention to the task of rescuing the man. Should he be close to

another vessel which could more easily rescue the man, a request for assistance should be made which may not be ignored. Should the master of the vessel himself fall overboard, it is the responsibility of the harpooner to see that the necessary rescue measures are taken, and the crew will be under his direct control. Any person who does not adhere to the above regulations will be liable to a sentence of solitary confinement of between two and eight years or, alternatively, exile for a corresponding period.

4. Whenever fishing vessels of different groups happen to be fishing within certain zones or in areas bordering on these zones, the fishing should be done in conjunction with each other and the catch divided between the different groups in proportion to the number of vessels in each group.

The fishing expeditions should be directed by the leader, master, or skipper with the longest experience, unless other arrangements have been made to the contrary. The leader, master, or skipper who violates these regulations will be liable to a fine of Esc. 500.00 to 2,000.00 [$17.75–$71.00] and a prison sentence of between ten to thirty days.

5. All vessels fishing in zones in which they do not have the right to do so lose the right to the catch from that area, which should be handed to the owners of the area, except in cases where the fishing is carried out under the terms of paragraph four. The owners of the vessel that fails to comply with these regulations will be required to compensate the owner of the particular area where the whale was caught with an amount equal to the value of the catch and in addition is liable to a fine of Esc. 5,000.00 to 10,000.00 [$177.50–$355.00].

The boundaries of the zones in the center of the Archipelago are as follows:

3rd zone [2]—Island of Terceira, extending to six miles from the coast.

4th zone —Island of Graciosa, extending to six miles from the coast.

5th zone —Part of the Island of Pico consisting of the part which runs parallel to the east of the island and the line to the southwest of Madalena, within six miles from the coast.

6th zone —Islands of São Jorge, Fayal, and Pico, with the exclusion of those parts pertaining to the 5th zone within six miles from the coast.

6. Whaling groups are forbidden to station their vessels in zones other than those specifically marked out for their use, except when adequate permission has been obtained from the port officials.

7. Should a whale be found dead or wounded in the sea or on the shore, the port authorities should be informed immediately. Failure to do so and any destruction of the harpooning weapon or other evidence will incur a fine of Esc. 500 to 2,000.00 [$17.75–$71.00] and a prison sentence of ten to twenty days.

8. Should the lines of two different whaling groups get entangled with each other, the groups should, unless by special authority, try to disentangle their lines without cutting them. Recourse to cutting the lines will only be permitted when either one or other of the vessels is in imminent danger or when this constitutes a danger to one or other of the crew members. Failure to abide by these regulations will be subject to a fine of between Esc.

---

[2] *It must be assumed that the first and second zones refer to the eastern and western extremities of the archipelago.*

100 to 1,000.00 [$3.50–$35.00] and a prison sentence of five to ten days.

9. It is forbidden to kill or harpoon whales which come under the category of *Balaena*, generally known as *Baleias Francas*; female whales which are still in the stages of feeding their young or the young suckling whales. The crew of vessels who are guilty of killing whales which come under the above category will lose their rights to a share in the catch, whether it be in the form of a percentage of the catch or a remuneration by cash. A recurrence of a similar nature will cause the master or harpooner responsible to be liable to a fine of Esc. 500.00 to 2,000.00 [$17.75–$71.00].

10. The crew are expected to be in attendance punctually when called for and to take part in the expedition for which they are registered. Exception can only be permitted for a justifiable motive. A member of the crew who absents himself without a justified reason will be liable to a prison sentence of up to ten days. The sentence will be doubled for a recurrence of a similar nature.

It will be seen that these regulations seek, among other things, to avoid danger arising from rivalries between crews; and rivalry between crews of different companies has always been very sharp and inclined to breed recklessness. But the competitive fire of the men is not limited by the ownership of the boats. There may be disputes even among the boats of one association. Every crew strives for the biggest catch, whatever other boats there may be, whoever their owners. And beyond the boundaries of the whaling zones, in the free water beyond the six-mile limits, all boats may meet and rivalry may be fiercely unbounded. Then, with the prize to the most daring, the authority of the most senior master may be a feeble implement.

The whaling zones referred to in the regulations were established in 1954, and the hope was that by their limitations they would cool the competitive fires of the crews. Until then, when all could fish freely, disputes were so fierce as sometimes to end in loss of life. No doubt those mortal rivalries have been reduced; but an intrepid boldness, a sea-wild freedom of action, had been so long in the nature of these open-boat whalers that the men find it hard to toe the stringent line of the rules. The strenuous urge of rivalry is there still, and it comes not only from the financial rewards of success; pride, professional self-respect, is deeply involved.

CHAPTER

8

WHEN THE hunt is done, when the killed whales have been towed home, they are brought to the factory to be worked up; that I have described in Chapter Four. The relative modernity of it is now universal in the islands. So it is now, but so short a time ago a majority of whales were still treated by methods that had not changed at all from those used by the New Englanders certainly as long ago as the mid-eighteenth century. It might be said to be "change" that the Yankee whalemen did their work from the deck of a whaleship, and the Azoreans did it by the shore; in this there is no true change, because the methods were transcribed intact from ship to shore, to the "try-works stations." It is so recently that the last try works passed from use in the Azores that the nature of their working is inseparable from this story. When I asked in Horta how long it was since the last try works ceased, they said, "Oh—about fifteen years." But that, I think, must have been an off-the-cuff generalization. Robert Clarke tells how, in 1953, in the whole

Azores there were only four modern factories with steam winches and pressure cookers. There were still eleven try-works practicing the old unchanged ways.

Among the first of the new factories was that at Porto Pim, at the edge of Horta, and still, just along the shore from it, you can see the silent, decaying remains of the try works that was its forgoer. In the quietness and the stillness there, the ghosts of its active past touch the senses strongly. It was, for its time, a sophisticated unit; it had a try house, roofed, strongly walled, in addition to its exterior parts. At a majority of the try works the whole treatment of the whale was done in the open.

This treatment was called "saving the whale," and it had two parts. First the whale was "cut in," which meant taking from it the blubber and the spermaceti of the ponderous dome of head; then they, the blubber and the spermaceti, were "tried out." That meant their cooking in iron pots, "try pots," to get sperm oil and "head oil," and it was this latter process that at Porto Pim was done within the try house, but at most other stations was done on the open shore. By the standard of the whale factories of today it was a wasteful process because it saved nothing but the blubber and spermaceti. The bones, the meat, all else, were lost; after the cutting-in, the stripped carcass was towed out to sea on an ebb tide and abandoned.

The New England custom was to range the whale alongside the ship and then, from a platform rigged out from the ship above the whale, to take the blubber in a spiral strip which was started at the flipper and continued to the tail. Tackles turned the whale in the water as the strip was cut and freed from the tissue beneath. So it was done at Azorean shore try works, with the whale ranged alongside a jetty or some such advantage, and usually with a platform rigged out from there above the whale. The whale, floating on its side, was made fast at either end to massive ring bolts in the quay.

Now, at the modern factories, the working up of the whale is done by the factories' men; formerly, at the try works, it was the whalers themselves who cut in the whale. Their instruments were cutting spades, of three kinds and similar to boat spades. The scarfing spade cut the blubber, and it differed from a boat spade by being wider in the blade. The leaning spade, wider still, separated blubber from adherent lumps of meat. The bone spade was bigger, with a heavy blade and a long shaft so that it could do such formidable work as the removal of the head.

The separating of the head seems invariably to have been a first or very early part of the work—as it still is on the flensing platform of the whale factory. Cutting in of the rest started at the flipper, to which a man would go in a rowboat, taking to it the very heavy blubber hook, inserting that in a place cut out by a cutting spade. There the scarfing of the blubber started; the way of doing it had some variation from one try works to another. At some, I have been told, there were derricks from which the heavy tackles worked, lifting away the monstrous blubber strip as it was cut. At the try works at Porto Pim it was so done, with derricks and massive hand-turned winches.

I think indeed that several details of working may have been different there; Peter, of Café Sport, remembers very well the busy time of its heyday when he, a boy with other boys, dallied there. No platform was rigged because a quay serving the same purpose was hewn from the rock where the skirts of Monte da Guia reached the water of Porto Pim bay. It had that amount of elevation that the men could conveniently do their work from it with no other aid. All the works there below the level of the try house were as impressively cut from the rock. Hewn steps came down from the little rough road above to the cutting-in quay, to another, smaller one for the exclusive cutting in of the head, and to a stranding place for whaleboats, with a boathouse worked into the rock. The bows of the boats, within the boathouse, were accommodated in boat-shaped recesses carved from the rock.

Just above the cutting-in quay, two winches were solidly bedded down into the rock, and from them the heavy ropes went to the derricks and thence to the tackles carrying the blubber hooks. Of these there were two, for alternate working. When the first had been inserted at the flipper, cutting began, around the flipper and up the side of the whale in a great parallel strip, five to six feet wide. The men labored at the winch and the gargantuan peeling strip, sheeny black and fondant white, was lifted from the carcass; as it lifted, the whale turned in the water to allow the extension of the strip around the body.

When it had gone so far that the blocks of the tackle had come against each other, a man standing against the up-reared blubber would cut a hole in it, and into that insert the second blubber hook. Then, above that, he would cut across the strip with a kind of long-handled sword, a boarding knife, and that first piece of strip was lifted onto the quay, "boarded," as they said. Now, with the second tackle lifting, the men cutting, and the whale turning, the peeling continued; so, turn by turn with the tackles, the peeling strip went continuously down the body till it reached the tail. There it was cut off and, soon, followed onto the quay by the amputated tail and flukes. Above the quay a crane hoisted the blubber on its way to the try house recessed in the flank of Monte da Guia.

That was the way of doing it at Porto Pim—or, at least, it was broadly the way of it. It is possible, and even probable, that I err in some details, because my information had to be had by conversation with those casting back in memory. And this was specifically the working of the Porto Pim try works; at some others in the Azores, for example, it was the custom to strand the whale on the shore and there cut it in, and then, obviously, not by the method of spiraling that could be done in water.

There seems to have been variation from station to station for the working of the head, and of the method at Porto Pim I was able to gain only a generalized idea. The place for it was a small harbor recessed into the rock below the try house, with a ramp in the rock going to the water's edge. Appearance suggested that the head would be hauled up there, but it seems that it was hoisted up-ended in the water and, so suspended, cut in. The men with their spades separated the case and the junk from their attachments in the head, then separated case from junk. The junk was pulled onto the ramp, and sometimes the case too, if it was a small one. More normally, I think, it was opened still up-ended within the head, and its contents of spermaceti bailed out. The means for that was the case bucket, wooden, with a rounded bottom. The lower jaw was saved so that bone and teeth could be used for scrimshaw. From the ramp the spermaceti was taken to the try house by a flight of hewn steps.

Within the try house now, all was heat and smoke and smell and busyness. I, who have smelt the relatively clinical whale factories, can guess well the thickly nauseous hang of smell there must have been there then. The black smoke, fat-laden, rolled from the boiling try pots.

So it was anyway when "trying out" had started; but first the blubber was prepared. Before it could go in the try pots it must be, as they said, minced. The blanket pieces, those lengths cut from the peeled spiral taken from the whale, were brought to the try house and cut into horse-pieces, about eighteen to twenty-four inches by six to eight inches. Those were "leaned up"—cleaned of adherent meat —then carried by "blubber pikes" to the mincing horse, a sturdy plank. There they were cut into "bibles" (or, sometimes, "books").

It was from the manner of their cutting (or mincing) for better boiling that they had their name. On the mincing horse they were sliced from the inner surface outward, with each cut stopping short of the outer surface. Thus each piece became like a book with about forty leaves, each half an inch thick. So cut, they were tumbled into the mincing tub beneath. From there they were pronged to the try pots with blubber forks, two-pronged, about seven or eight feet long. Now trying out would begin.

The try pots were iron, caldronlike; they were set in pairs in the ovens which, inevitably in the Azores, were of volcanic stone, covered over on the outside with cement. Under the try pots were the fire places, the "arches" in the old New England jargon; in them for fuel went "scraps" or "crackling," cooked dried-off remains of outer surfaces of "bibles" from previous trying out. They burned fattily, smelling evilly, gouting a heavy black cling of smoke to the one big chimney rising behind the stove. As the blubber cooked, seething in the pots, it was stirred constantly so that scraps should not burn and spoil the oil by darkening it. When the outer parts of the books, the spines, so to speak, became crisped, became crackling, cooking was finished. The scraps were taken out and fed into the arches to keep the fires going; the oil, boiling seething amber, was ladled into coolers beside the try works.

That was the general pattern, whether in the relative

luxury of try houses or the very common practice of trying out on the open shore. From the fragmentary information I was able to gather, I think the try house at Porto Pim must have been spacious and almost splendid by the common standard. Now, after long disuse, it stands foursquare and strong under the upfling of Monte da Guia; its massive walls of volcanic stone show little degeneration from neglect. It looks as if it could, upon any day's demand, pass straight back into its old activity.

Robert Clarke, writing of it, says that it housed two try works, two units, each one in the charge of one man; but as I was told of it there, three men worked, each with

his own try works of two pots. Perhaps the differeing accounts relate to different periods, perhaps memory erred.

As I was told of it, there was, along the rear wall, one try works and blubber pots; along each of the side walls there was a try works with its own blubber container. It was Peter who told me of it, told me of how he, as a small boy among other small boys, used to be drawn there when a whale had been cut in—rather, I imagine, as I recall the invincible magnetism of shoeing forges in which, as a boy, I spent so many nostalgically remembered hours.

The word would get around, he said, that a whale was being cut in, and he and those others would make their way across the gritty strand beneath Burnt Mountain. Past the little road, track really, to the try works they would go, and up the steep flank of Monte da Guia, clambering up the little hanging fields till they came to the thickets of faya bushes. Faya, Peter said, has sweet-tasting berries, and they would gather them, stuffing their pockets. Then they would come, stumbling and slithering, down again and past the cultivated patches to take a few sweet potatoes and ears of corn. All this was of a pattern, and who knows how many generations of boys before had gone as they went then, down to the try house?

There, by this time, the blubber would have come; the try pots would be seething and the oil clear and golden. The boys had cut for themselves small rods or sticks, and to these they affixed short links of wire for suspending the sweet potatoes and ears of corn. "May we," they would ask one of the men at the try pots, "do our cooking now?" "Oh yes, I suppose so," the man would answer, "but save me a pair won't you?"

So there they would stand, dangling the potatoes and corn in the boiling whale oil, and it is easy to imagine the cozy fascination and the companionship in the heat and sizzle. When a split opened in the sweet potatoes it was a signal that they were cooked; and, Peter said, they were delicious, with not the smallest taint of whale. I, watching the light-brown twinkle of his eyes, could see clearly those long-gone summer dalliances. That happy summery ghost of Peter's past helped to people the place, smoothe out the seams and fractures of its long desertion.

For twenty-five years or thereabouts the place had lain forsaken, and that time had left its scars, with winter's seas

and ocean winds. But the ghosts of so much past are
tenacious; I could still sense shades of all that old trafficking.
I stood with Peter, and he pointed to the bank above the
track, shaggy now with overhang of grass; there he said the
men's wives used to come, bringing meals. The men would
sit there to eat, for a time free from the try pots. Looking
then, we found old fragments of china, pieces of plate, blue
and white, debris of those long-gone meals. My mind's eye
saw them there; those sea-browned men in white, blue-
striped, bed-ticking pantaloons patched and over-patched,
laughing from under broad brims of straw hats, with cal-
loused spread of bare feet above the track. Now, a hundred
yards along, there is the whale factory with its tall chimney.
That much change there has been.

CHAPTER

9

TH E   D A Y S came and passed and added up, a desultory
sequence. They fell, one by one, victims of contrary weather.
First seep of light each morning woke me more suddenly
than any bell's outrageous summons; the nag of thwarted
expectancy sent me to peer at sky and wind and sea. The light
came slowly, lifting from the dark perimeter of horizon till
I could see the inky shape of Pico, the sharp-cut sea facets,
see the newly planted stripling trees on the Avenida, by the
water. A calm flat oily sea, a placid calm I hoped for, the
clear easy sky that would make good whaling weather. But,
so many mornings, the dire consequence still held; the
rumpled sky had the same cloud's tatter, the little trees still
writhed under the wind. The sea, those mornings, was often
gray, showing dully glinting facets like lead gashed, with a
windy spume of dull white in the half light. So it seems
now, harking back, a persistence of dark dour days; but indeed there were gayer days between, days when the sun was
brilliant and the sea as blue as gentians. There were even

calm days when hope exulted, though, more often, there was wind canceling chances on fine days or dark alike.

But whatever the morning, whether a little promising or beyond any reasonable doubt of promise, the constant compulsion drove me. While dawns could come at all they must find me at the harbor; what kind of calamity would it be if, on some unlikely day, the miraculous should happen, a blow raised, and I not there? So on wild rumbustious mornings, on mornings of golden lift of sun, on every morning fine or foul I hastened the Avenida's length in the pallid pause before the sun's rising, past the old Spanish fort, down to the harbor.

Then, morning by morning, there was the hardly varying pattern; Abílio Bettencourt would come first, check the engine, and José Vicente tidy again the impeccably tidy order of the launch. The fishermen would land their catches, gossip their interminable gossipings, have their brief fierce gusts of argument, and all would look at the sky, shrug, screw shoulders, and turn wry faces to the weather. *"Não baleia hoje"*—no whale today—they would say, smile regretfully, purse lips, spread expressive hands.

Full dawn would come, radiant or lowering, and I would wait, pacing or standing, trying to will the weather to stillness while the morning grew slowly. People gathered and the morning's first ferry to Pico, to Madalena across the five-mile straits, would throb to life and draw its white wake across the harbor. Then Peter would come, open the door of Café Sport, and it was full day. So it was, day after day, and each day I would start tensed with the prickle of readiness for the crisis that surely this day must bring; the days ticked off and it did not come and I not daring to leave the harbor. I loitered at the little tables of Café Sport, with the sparse food bag ready—bread, cheese, rough red wine—and there was sympathy there. "You are unlucky," they would say. "Bad weather for *baleia*," and they would ask me to have a glass of *azeitão* or *verdelho* to be solace for frustration.

Then there was that morning that was like some of the others, not one of the wild and overhung kind, not very windy, and with the sun intermittently shining through the cloud. At half past five I was on the quay in a cold fidget of expectation, because the weather had a little promise, and not till eight o'clock had the edge of nervous hope dulled. In Café Sport it was as other mornings were, long and idle, with gossip around the tables, and, I remember, there was a jocular dalliance with Peter on the pavement outside. Above Café Sport, in the flat there, a family lived that was forever at the windows, sitting between the shutters to watch the passing of the world. There was mother, short and stout and swart, and children whom I never counted accurately; and there was she who was probably daughter, swarthy as a brown olive and as roundly shaped. To her Peter called, mock-gallantly; his friend from England, he declared, was as much slave to her beauty as he was.

So, idly, the morning came to noon, and all expectation had gone from me. Then, suddenly, out of that infinity of deflation, suddenly shattering all ennui, there was a shout, exultant, tremendous, many voices.

"*Baleia! Baleia!*" the shout was, and when I, unconscious of volition, had exploded to the door, there they were on the quay, waving their arms, calling to me, shouting "*Baleia!*"

Here it was then, at last the trump, at last the blood-firing belly-chilling summons. Peter was shouting "*Baleia, go on, go on, baleia!*" And he was pushing into my hands the food bag, pushing me by the shoulder. Then I was going down to the quay, to the launch, running, though there was but two minutes' distance to go and the launch still fast at its moorings. As I came there, as the launch's engine burst into throaty life, there was the rocket.

It rose into ascent from the whale center's roof, hissing up, tracing its smoking eccentric vertical against the sky, suddenly stopping time, halting the fevered sequence like a still frame in a moving picture, as if all was caught in a perpetually suspended second, halfway in action. Then it had burst, a brief minor thunder, echoing beyond and beyond, with dark fragments in lazy parabolas in the sky, and action had returned.

Out of the little street from the whale center a dark clot of men extruded, ejected as if at a pinch on the street, and being out separated and became apart and running, shouting as they came *"Baleia! Baleia!"* One of them, I saw, was

José Rufino, and there were others whom I knew, whaleboat men and launch men, and as they came near, running, shouting, I saw the burn of cold fever in their eyes, the taut tense jut of jaw muscles. Now we were all caught in the elated shudder of fright, all lifted on the exultant tremor. I could feel the belly's cold tremble and the high-pitched twitch of muscle tuned beyond normality. Then we were aboard the launches, *Cetaceo* and *Walkiria*, crowded in their wells, jostling against the oil drums and the whale lines, and the moorings were cast off and there was Peter waving from the quay as the heavy roar of engines threw us under way across the harbor.

We surged past the moorings, past the American yacht with her elegant tumblehome, past the tuna boats and the pilot boat and under the light and out of the harbor. Now there was relief, the stretched brittle skin of tension eased because there was action; the bristled stand of nerves softened and lay back a little as the men took out cigarettes and smoked with staccato movements.

The launches roared on, following the circuit of the coast, going under the beetling of those lowering precipices, past the jagged jut of headlands and the surf-lined bays, roaring on to Salão. Now there was a unity aboard, an understanding and cohesion without the speaking of a word, with eyes in proxy for mouths clamped close. I found the eyes of a young man, lean, dark, wire-strung, fixed on mine. His were dark, black-rimmed, with white below the iris; he smiled faintly without a muscle's movement, and we were close, as men in danger are. The sun's intermittent gleam had gone; the sky hung obscurely. The swell rose and shattered against our plunging bows.

Then we had rounded the last snarling thrust of headland and there over the bows was Salão; and waiting on the roll and pitching break of the swell were the *canoas,* a frail cluster under the jagged toss of rock. We came up on them and I could see their crews, looking wild there under the dark sky and the high threat of cliff, looking wild and piratical as these men do, these tranquil and tempestuous men.

Now there was the nervous ordered haste of whaling, the making fast of tow warps, we in *Walkiria* first because we were the faster boat, then *Cetaceo,* and the engines' roar rose again, the wakes streamed out and the coast dropped astern.

The bearing was a little east of north, and we were making fifteen or sixteen knots; Pico came up to starboard, deep-blue and towering with the pale splatter of Madelena dropping to the sea. On their straining warps the *canoas* bounced in our wake; their crews were clustered aft; across the seeth and boil of wake between I could sense the tight tension of them. Astern, losing distance, there was *Cetaceo* and her tow of *canoas,* appearing and vanishing in the roll of the swell. The radio barked and shouted, instructing continuously, amplified above the engine's uproar, guiding, correcting, with Abilio making his calling two-note whistle, checking course. Pico's soaring summit had gone now, lost in the pink-shot vaporous hang of blue, and over the shoulder of Pico there was the translucent smudge-like settled cloud that was São Jorge, long and umber-mauve, half-defined between sea and sky.

The men, crowded forward in the wheelhouse, were talking quietly now, mouths close because of engine's clamor, short clipped words dropping out below the knit of straining brows and taut eyes. Beside me there was a whaleboat man; he smoked continuously, and I saw the hard twitch of his jaw. There was the sense of danger in the boat, but not now fear of danger but its sharp raw-edged uplifting. There was too much time, too long a going for the first cold thrilled quake to last. The raising of the blow had been far offshore, and our going came up to a first hour with Pico softening on the starboard quarter and São Jorge enlarging and lengthening down the far sea distance. The hour passed and time grew and the second hour was accumulating with Pico astern and faint now; and now, to the radio's command we had changed course a few points, out of the east to due north, with São Jorge losing substance again, growing low and faint and amorphous mauve.

Walkiria still forged on, bucketing over the swell; Pico had become a wisp and was lost under the stern, São Jorge only a low recurrent wraith between the swell's lift and fall. *Cetaceo* now was far astern, showing on the crests, swallowed in the troughs. Then São Jorge was no more; there was nothing but the sea ahead and the faint smear of Fayal astern and the huge oceanic loneliness. It seemed to me then a queer fantasy that the lookouts ashore could discern, identify, and so closely locate the blow of a whale in that immeasurable heave of sea. But *Walkiria* raced on purposefully, with the same undiminished seeming of certainty, driving on to the radio's constant stutter; I remembered that it is seldom that a blow once raised is lost—seldom is the whale not fastened and, ultimately, killed. There seemed no thought in the men that one whale in so much sea could be lost; the high twang of their tension was as sentient as if the whale was visible before the bows. I had begun to feel that this was a voyage into a nerve-wracked eternity.

And then suddenly we had stopped; we were near the whale then, within a mile of it. The engine was in neutral, purring gruffly, and we rolled in the sudden quiet; Abilio was consulting his radio. There was a new feeling in the boat, a different intensity, a forming up, ordering. I, waiting, could see nothing but the huge empty horizon's rim and *Cetaceo* now coming up on us. I had a sense of all time gone, all gone, nothing but eternity in that enormous vacuity—but with the consciousness of entanglement, inexorable now with event's appalling course.

A *canoa* was hauled up on its warp now, up to *Walkiria*, bringing its bows alongside; from the stern there came the stroke oarsman, picking his way over crammed gear. He came aboard *Walkiria*. So, for me, a place had been made in the *canoa*. Though the danger of the hunt so overhangs, though the part of each man is so pertinent to the safety of all, in their great courtesy they had given me this place. In the heave and lop I climbed over *Walkiria's* gunwale, felt with tentative feet, dropped into the *canoa*, and teetered down the bouncing dancing craft to the stern. There, at the feet of the boatheader, I found a space of not much more than inches.

He was formidable, this boatheader, big as Azoreans go, broad and tough, heavy-shouldered, with blue eyes like sea reflections in the leather-brown of his face under the wide brim and high crown of his straw hat. His legs and feet, nearly at my eye level on the standing cleats, were large, knotted below the rolled legs of blue-striped pantaloons. His feet were pedestals, strong, spread, a corrugation of leather above, horny-thick below. He had almost an air of ferocity, a fervent swingeing air of piracy. Poised on his cleats, high and uplifted, he had a sort of rough majesty.

The tub oar, my neighbor forward in the boat, was elderly, lean, big-boned, brown and textured like a nut. He too wore the high-crowned straw hat; the eyes that looked from under it, half smiling, a little shy, were gentle and experienced, eyes that had seen much life. His eyes were blue and, as detail will impinge in such scarifying moments, I saw that they were faded round their edges, as if much sea searching had drawn the color from them.

I thought that now was the moment, now we would cast off our tow, now the men would bend to the great oars, the hunt begin. But *Walkiria* burst to noisy life again; the warp snapped taut. We were in tow, with the boatheader on his standing cleats scanning ahead, commanding *Walkiria* with shout and sweep of arm. A ferocious splendor had come upon him, an appearance of enlargement, a combustion. "Bear to starboard," his wide thrust of arm commanded, and he roared and imprecated at *Walkiria* as she strove to his directing. The high angry flood of words poured from him; he flung up a sinewed spread of fingers at the sky, shook his head like the rolling of a planet. The colored torrent of his words, a cindery gout, scorched across at *Walkiria* while the blue fire of his eyes searched ahead. So we went, searching, veering, bouncing in *Walkiria's* wake; half a mile away I could see *Cetaceo* and her tow of *canoas*, she too beating about, searching.

The hoarse vituperative roar of the boatheader continued, bludgeoning *Walkiria* to his bidding; then I saw his eyes fasten, seeming to contract. In the midst of his thunder he dropped his eyes to mine, with barely perceptible nod and smile, a brief sudden friendly private signal. He had raised the whale. His voice rose to crescendo; his arm's sweep ordered the casting-off of the tow. Suddenly then he relaxed, softened; he turned to me, rolled his head widely. "Eeeee— *caramba!*" he said.

Walkiria veered away; distance soon soaked up the sound of her. We lay rolling in the immensity of quiet. There was a change in the boat. There had been engine's roar and churn of water, tension's release in angry shouting; now there was this envelopment of quiet, the soft sound of water,

the transfiguration of the boatheader. There was none but
him and his crew now; he spoke softly, nearly whispering,
directing the intense, almost-silent activity, directing like a
gentle father. A soundless excitement wrapped the boat, a
sort of elation. The harpooner had come aft, to midships,
to tend the line, bending the line from the waist tub to that
from the after tub, and that to the box line of the harpoon.
His movements were tight, nerve-strung, his face hard-set,
but his actions precise and certain. He was a young man,
lean, wiry and tendony as a thorn bough, pale now, with
blue eyes hard under knit of brows. Then he was ready,
with first and second irons to his right against the thigh board;
all was ready, the long oars out, the boatheader on his
cleats with the great steering oar. The men bent to the stroke,
a long easy powerful stroke; they were smiling, smiling
inwardly, quietly, with intently absorbed eyes. I was conscious again of an elation, tightly contained.

One of the crew was young, a boy, eighteen perhaps,
brown-skinned, brown-eyed, still smooth with youth. Beyond him was one, probably twenty-four, who was darkly,
piratically handsome, with long dark face and great black
eyes under ebony smudge of brows. His neck was long,
wide-based, rising like a column to a fine curve of jaws.
Under his black line of mustache his teeth were white and
strong, a little parted with smiling.

They rowed, driving forward, and I had no consciousness
of direction in all that roll of sea; the boatheader was above
me, laying his weight to the steering oar, blue eyes peering,
scanning the dark heave. We were alone, no boat near; recurrently I saw one other of the *canoas*, showing for moments
in the sea's roll, and there, distant, showing often no more
than mast and wheelhouse, was a launch, and I not able to
know if she was *Walkiria* or *Cetaceo*.

Then the boatheader looked at me, nodded, pointed

with his head beyond our bows. He spoke quietly to the crew, one word. *"Força,"* he said.

Still, to my searching eyes, low in the boat, there was nothing, nothing but the immense horizon-rimmed dark-green heave of sea. But I knew, all knew, that he, upraised there, had seen the whale, seen it rounding out. Fear was gone now, only this high-strung elation; the men quickened stroke, straining to it, smiling. Only the harpooner did not smile. His face was rigid, stone-set.

So we went, forging, in that queer pregnant silence—and for how long I cannot say; there was no more time, moments or hours not divisible, with the boatheader looming like God on his cleats. Away to starboard, a mile perhaps, I saw a *canoa,* and it was hoisting sail.

Then there was a softening in the boatheader, a sort of declining, and I could interpret his minute gesture of head to me; the whale had sounded. How, in that huge oceanic enigma, I wondered, could men divine its unseen course?

The boatheader spoke, ordering softly, to Manuel, to José, to Fernando; all were silently busy, precise and certain while we rolled in the enormous empty enclosure of sea. Oars were boated, the great steering oar taken in, rudder and tiller mounted. Now the men were stepping the mast—and how, I wondered, could that great spread of canvas be hoist and we not capsize under the bellying of it? But the sails rose, the mild wind took them, and we as one leaned at the starboard gunwale. Now there was that sort of serenity that sailing brings, overlying the interim's pause of deadly excitement. We sailed, careening gently, with no sound but the bows' lap, beating the conjectured bounds of the whale's area. So probably for a mile we sailed, then went about, went on the other tack, went to the port gunwale with our weight.

But still there was no raising of the whale, no sharp poignant cry of *"bloz!"* We were utterly alone now, no sight of any other boat, no *canoa,* no launch. A sense of an eternity was strong in me, a sense of smudging out of half-remembered life before, of no conceivable firm promise of future. We beat up and down that unfeatured waste of water and there was nothing.

Some moments of communication may have no need of words; the time came when I felt the release of last tension from the boatheader, when I felt his quiet slipping into admitted tranquility. He looked at me, then smiled gently; he shook his head slowly, as if with submission. Then I knew that this was that unusual event, a whale lost.

And now I realized that we had come to evening, that I had not eaten since early morning, that I was hungry. I took out my food bag, that bag that on shore had been casually considered enough to keep away the worst edge of hunger for the length of a sea day. "You can live for a day on dry biscuits, can't you?" Peter had said, and I had agreed. But how disenchanting the austerity of dry biscuits seemed now, and how dry they were in my reluctant mouth. In earlier days of waiting for the rocket's call I had had that which the whalemen take, bread and cheese, but had turned to the casual ease of these packets of biscuits. They were alum-dry; they refused to be swallowed.

The men had their food now, bread, cheese, slabs of *massa cevada,* their big wicker-wrapped water jars with the handle by the neck. My neighbor of the tub oar was eyeing me obliquely, with gentle tentative eyes. Then, for a second, he laid his wide oar-scarred hand on my knee; he offered me a big piece of *massa cevada.* I, seeing how big the slab he had, was grateful to accept. When I had eaten it he, bolder now, offered me another piece, and this too I took gratefully. I ate it and was content, and when he offered me another piece, refused it. But he, solicitous, pressed it upon me diffidently. Now the boatheader, who had watched, frowned quietly, reprovingly, father-fashion; with his hand he made a gesture of gentle forbidding to my neighbor. I had declined, his gesture said, I must not be pressed. Such is the sensitive courtesy of these tough danger-despising men.

The men ate, drank water with crook of finger in the jar's handle, the jar lying across the elbow of horizontally raised arm, and head tilted back. We lay in the sea and the silence and waited. There was no more to be done; the whale was lost and the hunt over. Now we must wait till the launch should

find us, take our tow. We waited and it was quiet and the men talked, still mutedly. The boatheader and my tub-oar neighbor conversed slowly, meditatively, all the time by glance and tiny gesture making considerate inclusion of me, but not too markedly, for fear that they should be intrusive. I, then, still had so near to nothing of Portuguese that I could not join them, but by smile and response of senses, understanding grew—and had we not lived together through those fevered hours?

At midships now there had come a merriment, fun bubbling up from under the dissolving of the sharp shell of danger. Those two, the young brown boy and the handsome pirate, had become, quietly, a life-and-soul in the boat; the latter, like the boatheader, transmuted by the danger's passing, had shed his piracy; there had come to him the same mildness, the same gentleness of manner. The boy and he joked, cross-talked, and whatever the matter of it, midships and forward were convulsed. The harpooner had sloughed his brittle tension; he leaned on relaxed arms, rolled easily with the boat.

So we lay, in a sort of bliss of ease, and I cannot say for how much time before Walkiria showed dark and distant and then came up on us. As she gave us the warp for towing, the young transfigured pirate came aft, smiled to me as if to apologize for our lack of common speech, and took from under my thwart a great roll of polyethylene. With it, impromptu, he made a tent, from midships to aft, to shelter us all so that, as Walkiria lurched into roaring way, we could huddle from the drench of spray. It was growing cold now, the heavy sky losing its light, the whole limitless sea uneasy with the deepening of evening. We in the stern, tub oar, boatheader, and I, soon relinquished our edge of shelter, surrendering to the darkening sea.

Now we were on a homeward course, speeding in the churn of *Walkiria's* wake; under the polyethylene the sound rose, joke and laughter, then changing. They were singing, those two, singing in a melancholy, queer, wild way similar to that called *fado*. It was a song of two parts, on and on, first one, like a sound of longing, of forlorn sweetness, then the other, answering. It was a song of sadness, of man and woman perhaps, of lostness. The voices went on, desolate speech and sad answer; there seemed no beginning, no end. The boatheader sat upright, swaying on the cuddy-board, eyes blue and sightless with inward distance. The tub oar sat with arms limp between knees, with eyes lost beyond the horizon.

The singing died at last; there was silence under the polyethylene, silence for minutes until the voices rose again. It was comedy now; comedy for two voices, a high, yelping, monkified dialogue, with a dwelling on unctuous rounding of syllables; it had a funniness beyond comprehension of the words. The tub oar and the boatheader chuckled and, chuckling, looked at me, wagging heads, half proud, half apologetic. "These boys!" their manner said, "these boys!"

For a long time the dialogue continued, and what its story was I did not know, though its funniness was apparent; but at last it flagged—there were intervals and at last silence. It faltered and ended because time passed and we went on and there was nothing but the sky and the sinking light and the hissing passing of the seas. Sometimes, far to port, we saw the momentary crest's lift of *Cetaceo* and her *canoas*, but the swell's fold took them again and all the world was empty but for the sea and *Walkiria* and us. Our wake glimmered dim white, and all the rest was a molten deepening limitlessness, like an immensity of flowing graphite.

Then out of that empty loom of loneliness the porpoises came. Suddenly they were there, a host of slipping satiny creatures, supple as water, making hooping movements in the swell. They showed first fifty yards off, then closed on us, alongside, going with us a hand's touch off, liquidly moving, violet-black. One I soon knew, that open-ocean, sea-wild creature; I felt the sense of conscious association, saw, as each parabola took it clear of the surface, the turn of its eye to mine. It and the rest were all about us, undulating and speeding with us, a friendly merry escort. They were palpably companionable, without fear, coming as close as sea and boat allowed, going with us as the miles fell away and the light declined. So they went till the low black shape of Fayal grew higher over the bows, took silhouetted shape and solidity, abolishing the sea's emptiness. Then, as if they could come no nearer to man's dry-land world, they took leave of us, left with a sense of farewell. The darkening roll of sea was lonely again. Night had nearly come, extinguishing horizons, closing the world to the range of *Walkiria*'s lights.

There was now no word, no movement in the boat; under the polyethylene there was stillness. Perhaps they slept, all of them but the young pirate of the morning. He sat upright, clear of the polyethylene, just swaying to the boat's roll, eyes fixed astern, in a waking dream. The long clear column of his neck showed pale in the dim light, leading to the poise of handsome head. A beauty had come upon him.

Fayal grew slowly, a blacker black in the enclosure of night; landfalls accrue slowly in returns from sea. But at last it was over us, the craggy pile of Salão, the boil and smother of the rocks. I had to leave my friends in the *canoa*, release the cramp of limbs, climb aboard *Walkiria*. In *Walkiria* there was engine's warmth, the excruciating luxury of wheelhouse shelter. Comfort began to creep into the chill of bones as we beat back to Horta, roaring back through the nearly sightless night till the rounding of the last headland brought the lights. The hoisting spring line from the deck to the quay's rough porous stone was harsh on cold hands, but there, just up from the harbor, was the shine of Café Sport's door.

"No whales," they said as I went in. "You are unlucky." And they gave me a brandy for my comfort.

"But hurry," Peter said, "better get along to João's before he closes. You must be hungry."

And now I realized, so I was—wildly hungry.

CHAPTER

～～～～～～～～～～

10

I T WAS July and a year later when I returned to Horta,
coming on the same eternity in a day from Angra do Heroísmo
and through the islands in the little ship. She, the ship,
this time was *Santo Amaro,* not *Espirito Santo,* but as small
and dawdling in her voyaging from call to call as was her sister. Eleven hours of passage they said there would be, and for
most of thirteen hours *Santo Amaro* took her sauntering way
in the hot blue dazzle, under the towering pile of São Jorge,
over to Pico, and came in the evening to Fayal. There again
lay Horta, beyond the gentian breadth of the harbor in the
bland shine of evening sun, as pale and perfect and mosaicked
under the upfling of the hills as I had remembered her. I
scanned the pastel serenity of her front—but where was Café
Sport, where was the little blue façade, sea-bleached, that I
remembered so well? About there it had been, just about
where that small wall, brilliant flag-blue, sung from its neighbors. But yes, surely, that *was* Café Sport, Café Sport bedi-
zened, Café Sport in a flaunt of new paint. It seemed almost a
violent clang of change.

But, soon, when I walked through the door, the year's lapse dissolved. There was new paint within, as without; but there in his inviolable corner, rolling, I could swear, the same cigarette I had left him with, was Henrique, unchanged, unchangeable. And there, inevitably by his counter, was Peter, light-brown eyes with the same twinkle, the same lucid kindliness.

As with Café Sport so with Horta; inconsequential changes had come, details of people and things, but Horta faced the deep blue of sea and sky and the shimmer of Pico's peak across the straits with the same tranquillity. The young sailor of the pilot boat, Apollo-beautiful, had gone, the Captain of the Port had changed; the family above Café Sport (I never did count how many there were) still watched eternally from their windows the passing hours. The tiny whaling-launch skipper (was José Eugénio his name?), with whom I had been at sea, had taken a shore job; but when the whale rocket sounded, they told me, he chafed, having to remind himself of the solid benefit for which he had made the change.

It was the evening after my return, when the sun had fallen to a mellow slant and Peter and I were taking the freshened air at the door of Café Sport, that he came by, the little skipper. He was walking with a group under the sea-cropped trees across the road when he saw me, and then he flung up his arms as he rushed to meet me. "Senhor Bernardo," he shouted, and, as we met in the middle of the road, at my waist's height he embraced me. While the fervor of our greeting lasted, and it was not brief, there in the road, the traffic waited politely.

Small changes, the little skipper shorebound, a few faces gone, some new ones—naval ones—come, small ruffles on the placid surface of Horta's life. All of consequence was as it had been; my year's absence slipped from consciousness but for comparisons.

"You were unlucky last year," they told me in Café Sport, "that was a bad year for whales. This year it is good—the days have come, one after the other, when it has been good whaling weather. There have been many whales killed."

And though now, just with my return, the weather became contrary, with the wind coming rough and strong out of the south, they said that would pass. It was no more than the change of moon, the passing of full moon; with that past there would be good whaling weather again with the wind from north or northeast and a calm sea, in just a few days perhaps. Then, in the way of Horta, they fell again to talk of whaling, and Senhor Silva told of that time, not many years since, when there had been a funeral at Cais do Pico. Whalemen carried the coffin, and as they went slowly, with proper sad solemnity, the whale rocket fired. Upon the instant they set the coffin down, there in the middle of the road, and they ran with their cry *"Baleia! Baleia!"* And there the coffin remained till the hunt was over. Such moments establish their own priorities where whalemen live in the Azores.

It was now, too, that I heard of the Fula family, men of Pico whom I had not known before. Under that system by which Pico whaling companies may have boats working out of Fayal, there was at Castelo Branco a Pico whaling station. There, the Fulas, immigrants from across the straits, were stationed in a sort of dynastic outpost. In benign headship was the father, elderly but still so full of heart and vigor that he skippered one of the two *canoas* of the place. From his seventeen sons came most of the crewmen of the two boats, and another son skippered one of the two tow launches.

They were formidable men, these Fulas, formidable and fine and typifying as well as any might the nature of their kind—simple, brave, modest men. They had that entirely un-self-conscious tacit bravery of their kind, an unquestioning stoic toughness, carried, in the Azorean way, within a pacific gentleness. I heard of them first from Bruno Vailati, who had come from Italy, as I had come from England, because he too could not resist a story of so strange a survival.

He had, he told me, been at sea with the Fulas. Early, at that pallid time between dawn and sunrise, the rocket had fired at Castelo Branco, and they had gone hours, thirty or more miles offshore, before they came upon the whale's blow. So it may often be, and if the harpooning and the lancing and the death should come soon, the boats may make their return at not too arduously late a time. It can be so with a whale not too warily nervous; but this one was elusive, sensing them perhaps, and sounding repeatedly before their approach. That may not be too great a hardship on a day of serving wind when the chase may be made under sail; this was a still day, one for rowing. The men pulled the great oars, strove at them, but, again and again, at about the time for boating the oars, turning to paddles for the final approach, the whale peaked its flukes and sounded.

So the attritional hours passed, with Fayal fading under the stern. Father Fula, high on his cleats before the cuddy-board, urged them to the stroke, whispering, stroke by stroke.

"Row hard," he said. "This is for all of us. Think of your families."

For five hours they chased the whale, for five hours pulled the oars with no seeming that they would ever achieve prox-imity. But, at last, they went on the whale, the harpoon was darted, the whale fastened. Even now there was to be no early end, no respite; though quite soon the first lancing was done, there was no weakening in the whale. It still ran hard, sound-ing, towing the *canoa*; again and again when it slackened the men hauled up on it till their hands bled. Repeatedly it was lanced.

The hours passed and the monstrous strength of the quarry seemed in no way lessened; the sun declined and the light drained, darkness came. Now it was half past eight or a little later (half past ten by the time of continental Europe), and the whale, which had been lanced at least ten times, did seem at last to be weakening perceptibly. So it seemed; but suddenly in an eruptive burst of strength it broke away. Ten hours in an agony of labor, ten hours of peril, and the whale was lost. The boat lay idly in the swell, the men sat slumped with riven hands hanging.

"Há armanhã,"—there is tomorrow—they said, when Bruno mourned for them.

He, telling me the story, said, "These are the finest men in the world, brave, simple men—and so poor, so terribly, pitifully poor."

That night they reached harbor at two o'clock; the day had been twenty-two hours long and the last six or so hours of it in dark and cold and a drench of spray. "But they were whaling again next day," Bruno said.

That first day after my return was a Sunday and a day of whalemen's *festa* at Capelinhos, so the lookouts were deserted, and the whalemen in their fine clothes allowed themselves the pleasure of a little drink in the cafés—though indeed, it is little enough of that that they can afford. At Café Sport the day passed in its old time-abandoned fashion, with hot blue hang of sky and blue glint of sea beyond the door; in the afternoon, when the shade came we, Peter and I, took chairs upon the black and white pavement outside to feel the air and watch the sea and gossip with those who chanced by.

And, in Horta, when it is Sunday and the sun hot and the shade cavernous under the trees, it is a time for promenade;

the family takes its unhurried meander, through the square by Café International, up past the Spanish fort and down by Café Sport to look at the harbor. They go, father and snug-plump mother and nut-brown children, till they come to the strand; upon its dark volcanic sand the children play. There is a placid bliss upon the afternoon, and who could think then of such raw drama as belongs to other days?

But this is Fayal, and through its greatest tranquillity there is always that fiery thread of whaling, and those who came by, renewing friendship, forgot their Sabbatical calm to talk of whaling and what might be my chances. The weather would change they said; in a day or two there would be the easy sea and the northerly wind; in two or three days perhaps, not tomorrow. And, the next day, Monday, the wind still blew out of the south and I took the interim to attend upon the Captain of the Port for the renewal of the "Death Warrant," declaring again as I had a year before that it was no responsibility but mine if I should come to death or injury while at sea with the whaleboats.

Next day, it was thought, there could be whaling weather; at four a.m., in the last dark, I was up, and a half past four out to Castelo Branco to be there when first light should seep up from the horizon. Out of Horta you take the coast road that sinuates its opportunistic way around the lofty flanks of Fayal, following its dizzy curves above the sea till you come to Castelo Branco. There, between white walls, you leave the road, drop down a steep fall of rock-paved track, down past the gardens, threading through the cling of little corn fields, falling away from the heights to come to the whale station. It, in the Azorean way, like Salão, is the merest notch in the coast's awful sheer, the smallest rock-girt cove. The frozen craggy tumble of old lava flow hems it in, crowds upon the boat slip, and it must be reached by a slipping half-run from the track above.

As I came there, dawn's first gray light was taking color, with a golden penumbra rising from the sea's hard distant blue-black edge. Then the light grew quickly, flooding up the sky, laying that half-unreality of early hours upon the fierce black seethe of rock. In this time between dawn and sunrise on cloudless mornings there is an interval of infinity, when there is no night, no day, when the possibility of drama to come has a thin keen queer stringency. In the still-hushed pause, not day, not night, what may come has an enchanted threat that the wildest events may not have by common day.

But the light swelled and enlarged, pouring into everything, pushing away the chilled witchery of the time between; then the sharp silhouette of Pico lost its edge in a golden blaze. The sun lifted behind the shoulder of the peak; suddenly it was warm, it was day, there was reality.

It was day, but was it to be a whaling day? The wind still came from over the heights, gentler now, but still from the south. The two tow launches lay moored to buoys just offshore, and with them the two *canoas* with their crews. And they now were coming to shore, paddling through the fangy mouth of the little cove and then grounding the boats and drawing them up the slip on the hewn-out wooden keel shoes. In the rock face was set a block and tackle, and with the heaving of the men and the creaking pull of the tackle the boats were brought up the slip.

The rocket's call was unlikely this morning then. Whalemen's wives and children waited at the track's end above; and I saw that every return from the sea is an occasion for gratitude, for welcoming back. They came climbing up from the slip now, the whalemen, these men of Pico, and that was how I first met José Fula and Antonio da Costa his brother-in-law. José, who was small and lean and sea-burnt brown under the wide shade of his straw hat, and with a wide sweep of mustache, was boatheader of his *canoa*. Antonio, short and broad and heavy-shouldered, was his harpooner; the two of them, tough and brave as ever whalemen are, wild-looking in their whaler's clothes, were shy.

Above, by the track, José's two daughters, nine and eleven perhaps, were waiting; they entwined his arms, either side. He, holding them, had a tenderness as if this was one more moment gained. Soon he and they and all the rest wandered away, going to such homes as they had there; we, Bruno and I, were left in the silent sunny loneliness above the sea. The day was growing now, half past seven and then eight o'clock; the sun was climbing up the hot blue arch of sky. We drowsed in the weight of warmth, still waiting on the chance that the rocket might burst upon the vast peace.

I wandered off soon, to look for ears of corn (we had not eaten that morning); I followed the track, grassy now, around the falling flank of land to the sea, against the boul-dery walls that held the terraced fields. It was so quiet in that blessing of sun, the grass so gently patterned with sun and shadow, the sea so huge and blue and infinitely at peace, that so bloody a drama as whaling was hardly conceivable. In a shade of trees I found a tethered kid, a softly bleating little goat that curvetted prettily, blinking its queer squinting hircine eyes, placating for its head to be scratched. Just be-yond I climbed up from the track through a twist of olive boles to take some ears of corn.

We made a little fire of gathered wood scraps, and what the wood was I do not know, but the burning of it was sharp, aromatic, delighting; when it had gone to a red glow of ash we cooked the corn. Eating that impromptu breakfast on the grass above the sea, the sharp pangs of our expectancy flagged. Hardly possible now that the rocket's summons would come. We lay there, in the huge peace, watching the idling grass-hoppers, fully two inches long. Then there came a tiny boy, coming from who knows where beyond the boat slip, and going on any guess of inconsequential business. He wore nothing but a short little shirt, and below that his little brown bottom and legs went with short nearly baby steps. He, remote in the privacy of his child world, did not see us. I wondered what absorbing summer soliloquy filled his year-long hours. We went soon; there was to be no whale today.

By nightfall the wind had changed; they were confident in Café Sport. There was Othon, Othon da Rosa Silveira, and Peter.

"Tomorrow," they said. "It will be good, good whaling weather. The wind is going round to north—the sea will be calmer, the lookouts will be able to see the blows. Better be up early, be at Castelo Branco when the light comes."

And, at four o'clock, I was out of bed as if ejected. As the stars began to fade, and the pall of night became translucent, I was on the road to Castelo Branco. There, when I came, there was expectancy; as the light rose from under the horizon the men came, José, Antonio, and the rest. One, in a fidget of eagerness to prove his usefulness, was a boy, fifteen, sixteen perhaps. The taut moments ticked off, not with the unshaped timelessness of yesterday, but with the sense of counting down to certainty.

But early hours are long hours; they built and grew by separate seconds, each tight with its hard anticipation. Five o'clock, then six o'clock, a taut millenium, and then seven o'clock; the summons had not come but certainty hardened with the seconds. At twenty minutes past seven there was the rocket, suddenly shattering brittle time. It rose from a house up the track toward the road, rising and rising, a white ascending pencil, while time waited. Then it broke, the cracking knell rebounding from the heights, sounding and resounding.

Before the sound had died we were pouring down, going
to the boats, going as by one actuation, going silently; there
was no cry of "Baleia!"—only the emergency's quick routine.
These were quiet men; there was nothing but the brief order,
the staccato shorthand gesture. The sequence of a thousand
whaling mornings was worn to polished practice; the boats
on their keel shoes came down the slip, were launched, and
we were going out, past the black threat of the rock fangs, out
to the waiting launches. They, with engines running, seemed
to take human mood, as boats may, counting the impatient
seconds. Each took the tow of one *canoa*, engines surged to
full voices, wakes boiled out, and the little cove fell astern.
From rocket to making way had been four minutes.

The blaze of molten sun, climbing up the still pallid east,
was over the stern; we were going due west, under the coast
of the island, toward Capelinhos. Pico, gauzy and towering

astern, had no substance, was nothing of rock or soil; it was vaporous, just color, rosy-fawn, just crowned at its summit with a small floss of white cloud. The sea, ultramarine, boiled and folded against our bows, turning over in a diamond dazzle of white; the *canoas*, riding the launches' wake, veered and swayed and became a rhythm. The men, crowded aft, silhouettes against the eastern pour of light, were still, as if carved there. So they had gone, all but the boy, times beyond their memories' counting, but their corporate tension, their supra-normality, was a sort of exhalation.

The launches surged on and Capelinhos came up on the starboard bows; the first hour was falling away. How far, I asked, had the blow been seen? More than another two hours they said, and as the first hour came there was the new volcano of Capelinhos on our beam. Already, in the year's lapse since I had seen it, that scarified red waste had begun to fructify. All over the sweep to the broken lighthouse that had been blank and arid there was a checkered pattern of *Arundo donax*—planted, I supposed, to hold and bind and regenerate. The volcano itself was as it had been, a rust-red sterile pile.

Now Fayal was dropping astern, now we were forging into that enormous anonymity of sea and sky, the blue sun-glinting emptiness with no shaping mark but its horizon. But the boats went unhesitatingly, full-throttled with arrow straightness in all that unshaped blue vastness of space, heading for a blow a few feet high, beyond the curtain of so many miles. We plunged on, and Fayal had begun to dematerialize, melt its tossing heights to rosy gossamers. "Another two hours," they said.

The second hour grew and was spent, and Pico was a faint pink point under the stern and Fayal a tender haze against the dazzle; but we surged on without a point's deviation, and the third hour was gone. When a fourth hour had poured under the keel and it seemed that all future must be the same pursuit of the inviolable horizon, suddenly, with no word, sentiently, there was a change.

The men were stirring, peering into the rumpled distance of recessioned swell; and now on each launch a man went forward and, monkey-agile, swarmed up the mast to stand on the bosun's chair for its better sweep of vision. They veered apart now, the two launches, casting about, knowing part by lookout's guidance, part by their perception so akin to instinct, that this was the whale's vicinity.

Then from our *canoa, S. João Baptista,* there came a great shout.

"*Bloz,*" they cried, and pointed, shouting, to our starboard bow; and, as the launch sheered over with a boil of wake, I saw it there, the stubby thick-necked vaporized mushroom of water. It was tinted in the sun, pale-mushroom color. It was about a mile away.

Now the launch had stopped; we rolled in a silence quieter for the soft purr of engine and lap against the hull. The *canoa* had cast its tow and in the same moment the mast was being stepped. In the elongated seconds the sail was hoist, lifting slowly, as things move in dreams, coming nearly to its top, hesitating, then filling with an audible slap. And now, perhaps half a mile away, the whale was blowing, blowing and moving slowly away from us, punctuating its progress by the soft buzz of its blow.

The men were on the gunwales now, facing forward under the belly of the sail, paddles digging with a rapid rhythmic beat, so driving the boat that it seemed to skim. And, still, the whale was there, having its spoutings out, moving leisurely in its private world that had no hint of danger, a serene idling monster in the sunny morning. The climactic moments were counting down, yards falling away to the final crisis that must bring disaster to men or whale.

The *canoa* was closing on the whale, the stretched hard seconds painful one by one; the exultant fear, the elation, was on the men, with all existence compressed. José Fula, in the stern, was on the standing cleats, he and the tiller one organism. They will go astern of the whale, I thought; they will go on it from behind, coming up on its flank, and the fear was there, instant by instant, that before they could come on it, it would round out, peak its flukes, sound. But it continued, dallying there, moving slowly, blowing and blowing again. The sound of it was like heavy surf sliding back from a shingle beach.

The *canoa* did not go on the whale from astern; it came round ahead of it, turned, went on it straight at the great bluff of its head. It was going on the whale *cabeça com cabeça*, head and head, that tricky maneuver, depending on the judgment of the finest part of a second if it was to be boat, not whale, that should live.

Now Antonio was standing, braced in the clumsy cleat, leaning forward against the tense thrust of leg; the harpoon was raised in the rigid lift of arms. The whale blew again and as the soughing surfy sound died, the *canoa* was on it, just turning past the head and Antonio in that moment doubling with his orgasmic plunging thrust. Suddenly, unbelievably, the harpoon was in, the whale fastened.

It was astern, just yards astern; it heaved up vast and dark, a wet huge shimmer of creature; then the great flukes threw up, making a shadow over the boat, and it sounded with the boat bouncing on the white seethe as mast and sails were lowered. The boat came about, the line was pouring away, a hundred fathoms, two hundred fathoms; then the whale had leveled off. It seemed to pause, then the sudden plunge of line wrenched down the bows and the *canoa* was going headlong.

It was a wild whale, brief and furious, too furious for very long fighting; the frenzy of its first run, many fathoms deep, took the *canoa* with fierce power, bows sheering the swell, spray fountaining. So it went, half a mile, then the line slackened a little, jerked vastly, slackened again; now the sea was erupting, a huge white boil, and the whale thrashing in the surface, blowing. It weaved there for minutes, throwing its monstrous erratic head from side to side, blowing, beating the sea to a cauldron-seethe.

Then the great flukes went up, painted against the dazzled shine, and it sounded. But not long now, not as deep; the line burned out, then slowed, slackened, stopped, rose slowly. The men were up, astride the thwarts and, rhythmically, were hauling, and José gathering line in the stern.

But the whale ran again, not sounding now, running in the surface, spurting, stopping, running again, tracing a staccato white of wake. Then it was turning, feeling the inexorable drag of line, going in a great spasmodic circle, arcing widely and brokenly around the axis of the boat. It had stopped, beating the sea in an aimless pestered confusion. The men were hauling again, and then had taken the line into the blow cleat, bowing on to the whale.

Antonio was standing, statue-still, a set spring against the thigh board, lance poised; I could feel the hard quiver of waiting muscle. Foot by foot, pull by pull the boat came on the whale; it wallowed, blindly tiring, uncomprehending.

The boat was close now, but standing by, waiting; the lethal thrashing of the hurt bemused beast was still too great. Then it had slackened and in the pause the boat came close, right in, from an angle aft toward the flipper till the bows touched.

In the second the waiting stoppered-down pain for action in Antonio was released. The plunge came from his feet, through thighs and buttocks. He jackknifed, doubled in the vertical plunge of arms and lance, driving the lance so that it entered up to the shaft.

In its gargantuan anguish the whale rolled away, beat of flukes and flippers sending a swamp of spray over the boat. Antonio bending with a thrust of knees and shoulders strained on the lance warp till it sucked free of the great body, while the men, stroking with the oars, backed water. The whale, seeking to sound, lifted its flukes, failed, and they slapped down with a crack like gunfire. It plunged, surfaced, beating the sea; the boat was a frail slip against the awesome smother. Then the whale had turned, running under the surface, coming under the boat so that it lifted, teetered on a three-foot crest of displacement. The whale ran, and line was pouring away again; two hundred yards perhaps it ran, then stopped and weaved and rolled indeterminately. The foam it made was pink now.

Now, cautiously, the men rowed up on it, José taking line, then slowed, waited; at the moment's opportunity they went on it again with Antonio poised against the thigh board. From two fathoms off he made his tossing dart, making the throw with a plunge of heavy shoulders. For long moments the lance seemed to hang, then dropped, entered, sunk for its shank's length. As the boat backed, as Antonio threw his weight to pull out the lance, a huge slow shudder ran through the whale. It rolled, as if in slow-motion, beat with flippers and flukes; then it blew. The blow was pink, a vaporized pink shimmer in the sun.

On the launch a shout went up; in the *canoa* a red waif was hoist, signaling for the closing in of the launch. The whale was beating around the boat, laboring, going in a huge slow inconsequentiality, blowing. The sea's clean blue was darkening, reddening.

The boat came on it again, not hesitating now; Antonio

made his throw again, and now suddenly, as with the bursting out of a stopper, the blow was opaque, not vaporized, but red and heavy with blood. With each sighing soughing gust of blow the blood came, spreading in the sea; boat and whale rolled in a sea of blood. The boat came again, lanced again, and after that again.

Now the whale was awash, surely spent. Its blow had lost its high plumy lift, was a low intermittent gush, an awful re-

current welling. It had begun to move in a great slow circle, a long labored perambulation, stopping, shuddering, going on. Once it lifted its flukes, slapped them thunderously. This was the flurry, nearly the end; the men waited.

Then suddenly an agony of new life seemed to come upon the whale; it lifted, half out of the sea, in an enormous pitiful convulsion. Its mighty flukes were suddenly up; it wallowed with giant frenzy of effort. It sounded.

The line poured away, going vertically, pouring down and down, a hundred fathoms, two hundred and another thirty. Then it had stopped; there was no more movement, nothing, just the dead fixed vertical of line. The whale had dived to die; there is no rarer event in whaling. It is the nearly inflexible fact that a whale will die at the surface.

Now, surely, this was disaster; could seven men lift that colossal corpse, a quarter of a mile below? But they sat quietly, relaxed upon the thwarts; they smoked, talked placidly. What would come would come. So we all waited, lying in the swell, waiting in a vast blue anticlimactic peace after such bloody drama, with *S. João Baptista* held and a little down at the bows by the vertical rod of line. So we must wait till help, radio-summoned, should come. Perhaps it was an hour, two hours, before we saw, minutely distant, two bow waves coming from the far haze of Fayal.

There was a tuna boat, seconded into whale service, and a launch towing a *canoa*. They came up on us and from the *canoa* went the crew into *S. João Baptista*, and from the tuna boat two more men—sixteen men in that light craft built for seven. And they then, without comment, without complaint, set to the lifting of the vast corpse, naked hands upon the wet raw line. With Antonio in the bows quietly chanting a rhythm, they began to haul, drawing shortly, foot by foot.

Where, I wondered, could men find such stoicism? How could they find faith in any end? Time passed, the swell rolled under us, and there was no sound but Antonio's soft chanting; the men became fixed in an hypnosis of movement —now with shortened draw, six inches perhaps. An hour fell away, two hours, then three hours, and still, now in mindless repetition, the men hauled, inching in the rigid line. Now their hands were bleeding; one had put socks upon his hands.

Five hours had passed when the whale became visible in the clear plunge of water, a pallid amorphous shimmer of shape in the blue. But there was no elation in the men, no triumph, merely acceptance—that and consideration of how, now, head and tail should be brought up together for the fastening of the tow warp at the tail. Twenty, perhaps thirty fathoms down lay the huge body.

Canoas on the slip notched into the jagged lava at Castelo Branco. José Fula is by the stern of the boat on the left.

The engineman of the launch, at peace for the moment, will discard his boots when action begins. *When the rocket has sounded in the first sun, the canoa is towed under the great rock at Castelo Branco.*

Ahead, half a mile or more, the blow has been seen.
The canoa *has cast its tow and the mast is stepped.*
José Fula is at the tiller.

The moment of crucial danger, lancing the monster—barely submerged a foot or so before the canoa's *bows. The whale's end is near and it thrashes blindly. The harpoon's shaft shows forward of the hump.*

Now the end, the flurry. The canoa *stands by,
waiting,* while the whale leaves its great circle
of *wake as it goes in a slow labor of death.*

The whale is dead, floating awash, and must be prepared for towing. A crewman grips the shaft of the harpoon while Antonio da Costa uses the boat spade to mortice a hole through the flukes for the fastening of the towing strap.

The whalemen's festa of *Nossa Senhora da Guia*. Down the rough road on *Monte da Guia* the procession comes bearing the figure of the saint. Many go barefoot as a gesture of thanksgiving.

*At the turn of the road on Monte da Guia: the blue
tranquillity of the five-mile straits across to Pico.*

Such a situation, however rarely, must have come before in the long past of whaling; but never, certainly, could its solution have been as it was now. Bruno Vailati, who was with us, is an aqualung diver; now he put on his heavy rubber suit, his air cylinder. He took a rope and he dived.

Then time became heavy with its burden of suspense, we scanning anxiously for sharks that, so often, are drawn by the blood of a killed whale. The incalculable minutes passed, and then there was Bruno, breaking at the surface; he had bent the rope about the peduncle of the tail.

There was not a man of us now not at the hauling; in the *canoa* the sixteen men, and on the launch the rest, and I wondering by what fortitude those men had hauled thus for five hours. We hauled now with doubled numbers, but the harsh line bit the hands, muscles of arms and back cracked to the gaining of each foot.

It was done at last; there was the whale hugely awash, a great gray heaving island of body, one so dearly won. Now it must be prepared for towing, and, at first, a hole was mortised in one fluke with the boat spade for the fastening of the towing strap. But this was a precarious tow, lacking normal buoyancy; towed thus it would have an angle to the pull. Then the strap, a chain, was fastened round the peduncle of the tail, and to that was bent the long towing warp; the two launches, in line, took up the tow. So they must go now, at two knots, regaining all those many miles eaten up in the frantic drama of chase and kill, a patient anticlimax for exhausted men. They would tow all night, coming about dawn perhaps to Porto Pim.

We now, emptied of everything, came gratefully aboard the tuna boat, learning that comfort is relative. There was space aboard, room to spread stretched legs on the forward deck, back against the wheelhouse. That, with a rolled sweater to absorb some of the deck's hard roll, was luxury. As it may be with such returns from sea—and the tuna boat was slow—the distant lift of land came to seem unattainable, forever the same soft distant smear beyond the swell. When we came under Capelinhos it was dark; the queer wild cry of the unseen sea birds was ghostly to our swooning senses. We had been five hours returning when at last we came to Horta and dragged ourselves from deck to the harsh stone of the quay.

It was next morning that we heard that the whale tow attachment on the launches had broken, that the whale had sunk and was lost. So many poignant hours of danger, such a monstrousness of toil; all that, in the end, for nothing.

11

THE WIND had veered again, back to south, and there were idle days ashore. The blow poured gustily over the peaks, smacking down; across the straits the white pile of surf was high against Pico. "But it won't last," said Othon and Peter, and on Friday evening the change was there, with a light wind from the north.

At Castelo Branco next morning dawn came quietly, with the sea's vista like a smooth rumple of blued steel. The surf creamed softly through the rocks, lapping the slip; there was a hardly breathing stillness. The men, already there, were spaced about like figures in a landscape, talking quietly, almost whispering; the sense of what was to come seemed to lie forebodingly on the hush. The apparent peace, the desultory quiet, had the sense of being poised. The minutes escaped, one by one, and then the sun's first blinding lances threw a blue blaze from the sea.

Exactly at six forty there was suddenly a hissing, a blowing gush of sound, like escaping steam, and for a hang of moments I could not identify it. Then as realization came, in the moment, there was the rocket's explosion; it had been detonated from one of the launches, not from shore. One of the men had been standing near, silently; now he looked at me, into my eyes with a kind of intimacy. He spoke quietly, hushed. *"Baleia,"* he said.

Now I was picking up my things—sweater, food—not conscious of movement; the scattered groups had coalesced, suddenly one, men with a common being, trailing down the slip to the boats. We slipped out, past the standing lava teeth, and the tows were taken. I noticed that *S. João Baptista* had only six men; the boy was not there. Perhaps the other day had been one to test him, prove his mettle. I hoped that there would be wind enough to sail that depleted boat.

We turned westward again, going under the white and massive sheer of rock that stands from the land there, disturbing the wailing hordes of sea birds. I, with an idling fragment of forward-straining mind, wondered if that rock, so fortress-like, gave Castelo Branco its name.

The sun was climbing now, a liquid blaze over the stern, and nowhere in the sky was there the smallest wisp of cloud to dilute the torrent of light and color. Capelinhos came up on our beam, and, as it dropped astern, we began to bear north of west. The western face of Fayal was over the stern, with Pico, translucent rose, on the port quarter. We forged on, turning over our wake like a dazzle of white lining to the ultramarine of the sea; we were on a course obliquely away from Fayal, with Pico beginning to disappear behind Fayal. When we were two hours out, Pico had gone and Fayal, alone in the whole vast bowl of blue, was softening under the stern.

How long now, I asked, when we had gone three hours and Fayal had become delicate with distance; it would be another hour they said. And, now, Pico was reappearing, showing on the farther side of Fayal, insubstantial fawn-pink on the starboard quarter. I judged we must have a bearing due northwest, and then to confirm it there was São Jorge, low and vaporous beyond Pico. The wind had freshened, with the long swell beginning to break against the plunge of bows.

The fourth hour had grown and was nearly done when men went to the mastheads to search the glitter of blue distance, though it seemed the same infinity of the swell's recession, as vacant of incident as the rest. By what apparent divination, I wondered, however good the shore direction, do the whalemen know the whale's vicinity? This seemed the same vast sea-loneliness as the hours gone, but in launch and boats now the men were drawn taut with expectation. I saw nothing, no blow, but the launches stopped, tows were cast off.

We were separating now, the launches apart on their searching and, with sails hoist and taking the wind, the *canoas* beating away. S. João Baptista went as if homing on a beam, bearing away on the starboard bow, scudding up the sea distance as if she had a certainty of assignation. I, in the launch this time, could watch the broad pattern of the hunt. Now, astern, there were other bow waves coming up, with dark smudges against the dazzle that soon consolidated into two launches with their tows. A quarter of a mile away they cast the tows—Fayal boats; I could see the yellow strakes of the *canoas*. One of those boatheaders, aloft on his cleats, must be José Rufino.

The boats' sails punctuated all the forward distances; there was S. João Baptista, a mile away, still going with the same conviction; I thought I could sense, across that blue mile of swell, the drawn elated tension in her. That was José Fula, that dark dot above her stern, and I thought of his sweep of mustache and how his gentle sanguine eyes would now be contracted with the sharp ecstacy of his hunter's peril. Another *canoa*, one from Castelo Branco I guessed, was keeping him close company, probably because where José went was not likely to be far from the whale.

I saw no blow, the sunny shift and shimmer of the distance dissolved so much; but I detected that the paddles were out on *S. João Baptista*. She had seen the blow, she was going on it, she was skating the sea like a wind-driven feather. We, in the launch, caught the shiver of the moment, straining vision to extremity, striving to see Antonio stand to the clumsy cleat. Then, there it must be—*S. João Baptista* had checked, yes mast and sails were coming down. Yes, she had fastened.

The whale had gone astern of her; she came about. She must have gone on the whale as before, *cabeça com cabeça*— there for a moment was the great smothery heave of sea, the gleam of sun on blackskin. The flukes went up, a second's silhouette, and the whale had sounded. I could guess the burning hiss of the running line; I could see the *canoa's* tossing on the maelstrom of the great beast's sounding.

The launch roared to life; we were surging up, full ahead till, 300 yards off, we stood by. The whale was running still, the twanging line emptying after it. Then it had stopped and time stopped until suddenly the sea burst white; there was the whale, the huge gray heave, the vast white toss of water. It blew and blew again; José had taken a turn or two at the loggerhead. He could not keep them; the flukes threw up again, the monstrous back rounded out. The whale sounded and the line was singing away again.

But the whale was lifting; there it was, suddenly, the eruptive burst and thrash of water. It paused and blew and ran again, going on the surface, making a boil of wake. And now José had taken turns at the loggerhead again, and the bows plunged and the *canoa* was towing, scudding in the whale's wake, the Nantucket sleigh ride, and we in the launch edging nearer, going with them.

So we went, a quarter of a mile till the flukes peaked again and the whale sounded and José must let go his hold at the loggerhead. The great pestered striving creature was tiring now though; in only minutes it surfaced, thrashing and rolling, and now I caught the sound of its blow, windy with distance, a softened gravelly sigh of sound. The men were up, astride the thwarts; they were hauling, creeping slowly on the whale.

Now it lifted its flukes, slapped them down, lifted them again, seeking to sound, but now with the beginning of an impotence upon it. In its confusion and anger it lifted its huge bluff of head, rolled it, and then was running again, snatching away the hauled line, towing the boat. It was staccato now, in a huge tormented bother, running, stopping, with intermittent lifting of ineffectual flukes. The men hauled, gave line, hauled, creeping nearer, coming with their midget brave impertinence upon that now languidly frantic quarry.

It was running no more; it lunged and rolled and beat at the surface. Now I could see its length, a gray enormity, sixty feet at a guess, an angry desperate giant, so direfully beset by a shadowy enemy outside its conception. It was making a lurching ambit about the boat now, a slow shaking circling, 150 yards off, blowing and thrashing and tired, but too threatening still for nearer approach. It seemed now to have fallen into a wild blind tormented anger, lifting and shaking its fearful head, lunging, throwing up and dropping its abortive flukes.

S. *João Baptista* meanwhile stood by, waiting, wary of this still-too-menacing monster, taking line when it slackened, but keeping safety's optimum distance. In the bows Antonio stood, arms hanging, patient for the moment of decision.

Now the whale had paused in its boiling circuit, lying in one place, thrashing still with flippers and flukes, but resting a little from its worst fury. I, in the launch, felt the nearly tangible tightening of emotion in the *canoa*. The oars were put out; Antonio, bracing and stiffening in the bows, picked up the lance. The boat moved forward, slowly, stroke by stroke, creeping on the whale. A renewed convulsion of fury came upon it, and the boat paused, blades out till the moment passed and the whale lay, quiet now, in a suspension of fatigue. Now the oars were in, stroking quickly, going fast on the quarry before opportunity should pass, Antonio braced in the thigh board in a forward-angled tensile poise against his thrust of left leg.

The seconds went down like audible ticks, painfully stretched, with the whale stirring and yawing and Antonio with lance in rigid readiness above his head. At almost the last second's drop, the whale humped, churned with flukes and flippers; but the *canoa*, too close for hesitation, went in. At two fathoms' distance, obliquely on the flipper, Antonio exploded, making his plunging tossing throw. The lance was in, the whale in awful frenzy lunging enormously away while the boat bounced crazily on the smother. As the men backed water two strokes, Antonio doubled, throwing back his weight to draw out the lance.

The whale was running, not far, not fast, beating and churning for two hundred yards, then stopping in its blind and baffled agony. It wallowed there, rolling its great head, blowing, while the boat waited with Antonio still at the clumsy cleat, lance in limp arms, relaxing, as the whalemen will, at any serving interval. Now the whale was moving again, in an aimless yawing inconsequence, trailing its turbulence, pausing and bursting in heavy gusts of movement. So it went, for half an hour perhaps an hour—how could I gauge time?—but all the time, too ferociously unpredictable, too menacing for the boat's approach.

Then its bursts of movement, its giant spasms of energy, fell away till it lay more quietly, just weaving, swaying head and flukes, beating intermittently with its flippers. The boat moved on it again, stroking cautiously, stealing up from aft outside the lateral cone of vision. It went so until, fifty yards off, seizing a still moment, it went quickly, going right in, "wood and blackskin." Antonio, poised and still, exploded from his feet, doubling like a spring released, plunging the lance to its shaft and then, in a gift of seconds, plunging in convulsive series—"churning" the lance.

Now the flukes had gone up, an awful canopy over the

boat, poised there a moment as the whale, stricken now, sought to sound and failed. As the boat backed water, gaining its own length of respite from the worst danger, the whale beat about in its gargantuan distress, rearing its head. Then it blew—the blow was pink.

From *canoa* and launch, from all of us, a great shout went up, and the whale had blown again, pink again, a pink foamy diaphany. And, now, the surfy smother of its wallow no longer dazzled back white at the sun; it too had taken the stain, a boiling seethe of pink.

On the *canoa* the waif was hoist, the red waif, and at its signal the launch came up to stand by; the end, if it was to come, had begun. It had begun, but it had no reckonable imminence; in its consummate pain the stricken beast seemed to find a vestige of its might. It could not sound, it could not run, but the anger of its agony, its stupendous distress, held off quick pressing of the end. It beat the sea, striving against its crippling, not seeming to weaken toward final vulnerability. So, sometimes, a whale may go on for indeterminate hours. Then, it must be a shared whale, cooperatively killed; now, at the summoning, the other *canoas* came up, that other one from Castelo Branco and two of Fayal. Now all of them stood by, all four, in a cautious encirclement.

So they waited, waiting upon a first interval of opportunity, and it may have been at half an hour's lapse that S. *João Baptista* seized a more quiescent moment to sever that sequence. She lunged in on a spurt of oars, and from two fathoms off Antonio made his tossing dart. And, as the whale rolled in a sickened recoil, as Antonio strove to retrieve the lance, José Rufino snatched advantage on the other flank, burying the lance to the shaft.

The gray immensity of wounded body lashed and shuddered; it blew with a thickened, sighing gush of sound. The blow was red, no longer vaporized, thickly bloody, an awful bloody gush.

Now the whale was truly in its preposterous decline. Though it fought still, still made vast convulsive movements, the more quiescent periods came oftener. Now it was blowing recurrently, a repeating bloody gush, and the blue had gone from the sea. Men and monster fought in a widening heave of blood. How, I wondered, could even that immensity of creature persist so pitifully in its remnant of life?

It had weakened now; its shuddering resurgencies came less often, but it was still dangerous, still with lethal capability. The boats were coming in continuously, coming in, making their darts, backing away. The lances went in again and again, but the whale still continued its prodigious labor of living, still thrashing the bloody surf. There was a Fayal boat that went on the whale, lanced, and, when the lance sucked free the shank was bent. But so immediately did the chance for another lancing come that the harpooner stopped in the straightening to dart again, driving in the bent lance.

Now the boats were shuttling, taking their rapid turns, and the whale's continuance had become a bloody nightmare. Its blow had sunk, the sighing gust of it fallen to a low surge. The lifted plume was gone; blood welled and pumped from the blowhole, canalling from the cleft and down the head, spreading viscously in the sea. It had become an outrageous miracle that it should still live.

A change came upon it; its beating died away. It had begun to move in a slow weaving perambulation. Then, slowly, it sank a little, the bloody wash of water closing over its back. So it was for minutes; then abruptly, explosively, its head burst vertically from the sea a full ten feet. It hung there for moments, the huge parallel of head; it opened its mouth to a gape, clashed its jaws. Then it collapsed into the sea.

Now the boats backed away, stood off; here was the flurry. With S. *João Baptista* as its axis, it moved in a wide circle, laboring spasmodically. Once it lifted from the water, half its depth, with a convulsion running through its immensity, then fell back in a beat of surge. Once it lifted its flukes, slapped them down explosively. Perhaps last life went from it then, perhaps it flickered on for a time. It still dragged its heavy course for a little longer, then lay still, motionless in the lift of swell, with one flipper standing rigidly. It was dead, "fin out."

Now a strange peace had come; all seemed spent, all time, all action. The drama was done; we lay in the long swell, blue again, the four boats and the launches strewn in a cluster in the emptiness, and in the midst of us the great lifeless gray undulation of whale. Then, like men stirring from a dream, the crew of S. *João Baptista* hauled up slowly on the line, coming up with another of the *canoas* to reeve the towing strap at the tail of the prize. It was all done so slowly, with a sort of lethargy of contentment, of freedom at last from danger and from striving. We, the rest of us, slumped where we were, loosely abandoned to the sea's roll.

The launches closed in; two of them were to take the tow, and I must go aboard another for the long hours back to Fayal —we were a long way off now. As it came alongside, a Fayal launch, its skipper, smiling, waved to me. It was Abilio Bettencourt with whom I had been at sea a year before; a queer reunion out of time and world.

The two launches, in line, began their two-knots tow that would take them out of day and through the night. We, with two *canoas* in tow, S. *João Baptista* and that of José Rufino, turned our bows to the low faint smudge of Fayal. The freshened wind had raised the dark-blue swell; it shattered against the yawing lurch and plunge of the bows, soon so dousing us with its drench that we were resigned. We sat in our saturation, waiting till the hours should pass.

I, lapsing into the soliloquy of such returns, thought of that pitiful giant, so pestered into death; and I thought of these men, so enduringly brave, so modestly stoical. The sperm whale, the persecuted monster, harms nothing—ex-

cept the giant squid on which it feeds. And the giant squid—what harm does it do to anything—except those creatures which are its prey? And the men, these whalemen; they are kindly, gentle men. They harm nothing, except the sperm whale by whose hunting they must live. I had seen indeed a small segment of Nature's remorseless cycle.

The land grew slowly, from vapor to firm substance; we came at last under Capelinhos, and after five hours were off

Varadouro. We put in there, bringing home José Rufino, his crew and his *canoa*; and, in this mellow aftermath, all went ashore to take a drink. Tomorrow was the *festa* of *Senhora da Guia*, the whalemen's annual festival. There would be no whaling, no dawn assignation, no peril. Already that sense of blissful pause that *festas* bring had touched the men. They smiled and were quiet, at rest for a while.

CHAPTER

12

*T*HE ROCKETS began quite early in the morning, poppling recurrently, a happy holiday sound, unlike the single foreboding knell of the whale rocket. In the streets the sense of *festa* was already there, a leisured lingering upon the moment, a sense, hard to define, of blissful inconsequence. People went their ways with a smiling tarrying air. There was luxury in the freedom to get up just when waking came, to take time with breakfast coffee.

But before I could give myself to the *festa's* easy peace I must go to the whale factory; there, this morning, would be yesterday's whale. As I walked, going in the early sun past the square and past the harbor and through to Porto Pim, there was such a gentle gaiety, such a festive play of rockets, it was hard to believe that the morning would see that monstrous butchery too. But at Porto Pim, when I came to the strand, the factory chimney was smoking across the little bay, the tackles were clanking. The water about the slip was bloody.

I went in at the gate and past the towering ordered piles

of *faya* wood for the stoking of the boilers; the clinging
retchy smell lay on the air, with a texture like cheese. It was
dim inside the factory, lofty and obscure, with the fatty hang
of fumes, shot with the lick of the furnaces. Beyond, outside
again in the blue morning brilliance, the flensing platform
had a sleazy shine of fat and blood; the bare-legged workers,
men and boys, pattered and paddled in the muck, larded
over with it. The boys, nut-brown under the blood, wore only
brief shorts over the beautiful knit of their young bodies.

A whale was nearly done; they were standing within the
emptied head, cutting up the skull with the great two-man
saw. The guts lay in the center of the flensing platform, a
quaking pile, red-brown and gray and gruesome yellow, a
ten-foot mound of matter. But this was not our whale of yesterday; that still lay below, moored to the buoy a little out
from the slip. It must wait until the first whale's waste had
gone.

I waited too, within the fetid flensing platform. Overhead
the sky was as pure and blue and sunny as heaven; beyond
the blood the bay dazzled back the blue, and the color of
waterfront houses lay under the lift of the hills. To endure the
smell I went from time to time to a high vantage on the wall
that caught the sweet blow of wind from the sea.

When they came to the clearing of the guts, cables were
taken from the winches and down the slip to pulley blocks in
the walls, coming back from there for purchase on the guts.
The grappling hooks were massive, barely within a man's lifting, and I wondered to see a man and a boy go to the handling
of them. The man was strong, heavy-chested and thick-
legged, and he braced to the hook's weight; but the boy, so
brown and smooth and elfin-slim, denied human mechanics.
Treading up the paunchy slither of coils, he dragged the hook
after him.

They set them, the two hooks, jabbing them into a quaking hold; the winches steamed and the pile began to move, shuffling on the miry stones, slipping and smearing down the slip to the water. When it was clear, oozily afloat, a dinghy took a cable from the pulley at the slip's end to the whale at its mooring. The cable was hooked to the towing strap against the flukes, the winch wheezed, and, slowly, the whale was brought to the slip. It was so huge and gray, so inert and rubber-smooth, that it seemed to have little to do with the living frantic creature that I had seen dwarfing the boats far out beyond the island.

The ponderous tackles were slid down the slip on the lubrication of fat and blood; the fastening of them was slow, interrupted by sudden flares of shouting and flinging of arms; if the pull should not be balanced, the whale would not come straight, would jam. It was done at last; the foreman ceased his raging, was suddenly easy and calm; with the winches steaming and chains clanking the whale came up the slip, the huge gray spread of flukes spanning all the width. It had not stopped before the cutting spades had begun, jabbing softly through the white fondant-textured blubber. I came away then; I had seen the end.

Outside the spangled air was soft; the clean wind came gently over the sandy waist of isthmus between Monte da Guia and Burnt Mountain. In the minute the stench and butchery bustle of the factory had sunk into the peace of the morning, a half-awareness in so much drowsy glint and lap of water. The first whaling *canoa* was already there, white-hulled with yellow strake, afloat on its reflection and easing in to be beached and drawn up on the strand. I stayed for a time, watching as the boat touched and the keel shoes were laid and it was drawn up with a slow care for its gay paint till it rested on its props. It had its flags, the little pennants overall, blue and green and yellow and red, and I, seeing it there, such a light perfection of elegance, could almost forget that the purpose which made it so had its bloody end at the factory.

Other boats were coming in, blue and white fishing boats, because on the day of *Senhora da Guia* they are blessed too. As I came up from the strand, under the white wall to the streets, people were busy in the sun, in a languid easy way, hanging the flags, decorating the fishing boat drawn up on the stones by the old Spanish water gate. I walked slowly through, toward the harbor, going in the mood of the day, and all the way the people passing and taking the holiday air at their windows were smiling and bidding me *"Bom dia."* The big doors of the whaling center were closed and locked within the incurving white sweep of walls; little girls in best satins and lacy frills played there, though with decorous care for their finery. There was the happy leisured suspension of everything but the passing of each sunny blissful minute.

The rockets cracked, the dawdling families promenaded by the harbor and soon, when I came to Café Sport, there were José Fula and Antonio da Costa, easy and at rest at one of the tables. And, when greetings were over, the intertwined arms, the embracing of shoulders, and the glasses of *verdelho* had come, there was José in a fervor of whaling talk, drawing with fingertip on the table. It was his way, he explained, invariably to go on the whale *cabeça com cabeça*. It was easier, yes, he said, to come from behind, to come on the flank where the blind zone is bigger; but always there is the threat of the upflung flukes—so many boats had been smashed so. But to come on the head, if the approach is well made, narrowly within the blind zone under the bluff of head, then slipping to one side at the moment of the dart, the fastened whale sweeps past and is astern before it peaks and sounds. There is little danger from the flukes then, and José, smiling and modest, could have made me think it as safely easy as going through a door if I had not seen the appalling need for a fraction of a second's exactitude in timing. A big bull's head may be thirty feet long, the teeth huge in its jaw, and just at the rear of the head is the perilous thrash of flipper.

But this was the day of *Senhora da Guia*, and for all the dreaming floating hours of it there was no danger, no stresses, no rocket's summons, nothing but the gentle gaiety and the peaceful popple in the air of the *festa* rockets. We dallied away the morning there, José, Antonio, and I, and even, for a time, they forgot whaling to talk of family and of home on Pico.

In the afternoon I went again to Porto Pim and under the ashy pile of Burnt Mountain, where the boats were drawn in a rank upon the strand. I went past the factory, quiet now, sunk into the universal placidity, and up the climbing twist of road on Monte da Guia. It was so quiet there, so submerged in summer peace and hum of insects that even the sense of the *festa* grew unreal, with the rockets' crackle soft on the drift of air. At the first turn, where the narrow track of road hangs over the plunge to the sea, the whole blue bliss of vista lay in the shimmer. There was Pico across the sapphire straits, without a fleck of cloud, soaring and sublime, blue-mauve, the hardly believable blue of sea and sky, the pastel sunlit sweep of Horta. It was so still, so serene with sunny distance, that such raw drama as whaling seemed nearly inconceivable; yet it was just such a day as this, were it not a *festa*, that would bring the rocket's call.

I went on, climbing slowly in that heat of afternoon, the drowsy sibilance of grasshoppers lulling the solitude. Then, around the last turn, there was the little church, *Senhora da Guia*; and now there was no more solitude, no grasshopper

silence. A throng was there, whalemen in stiff suits, women
in all their best satins. The children played and the bandsmen, in dark-blue and gold coats and white trousers, waited.
There is a form about the *festa* of *Senhora da Guia,* I know;
it goes its hallowed way from stage to stage, and so, no
doubt, it was going then.

But I could see no form, no pattern. The church was the
center, with high doors open, people passing in and passing
out, and I could find no order there. The church stood upon
its plinth, lodged on the hill's lip above the limitless blue
plain of sea, and there were broad steps up from the widening
of the stony road. On the plinth, on the steps, and on the
road, there were the people, just there it seemed in a smiling
sanguine dalliance of no beginning and no end. They sat
against the church wall, on the low parapet that enclosed
the plinth; they stood in groups and the children weaved
through all. There were two bands, and one of them was
seated with instruments against the church, waiting upon
that unchartable moment when they should play.

Going down from the church, down the steps, I found the
other band. It had been hot, climbing the hill, and I was
thirsty. I went to the little refreshment stand, so characteristically Azorean, that had been brought up the steep ascent by
no motorized aid. It was an elaborate, folding-out, ingenious
adaptation of a pedal tricycle, lavishly stocked with almost
everything that a drooling thirst could ask. And there I found
the bandsmen. They (and indeed many others) stood about
that little mobile kiosk, coolly splendid in blue and gold and
snowy white; as soon as I had gained the big glass of Pico
wine, I had been absorbed. Was the *senhor* enjoying the day
of *da Guia?* But he must be thirsty after the long climb;
please to finish his wine and have more. All was easy, placid,
and smiling, with no hint that life would ever have any event

again, ever anything but this timeless tarrying of wine in the sun and conversation. Others came to augment the bandsmen's care for my thirst; it became apparent that if time had withdrawn its aid I must save myself. When I had extricated myself, I returned to the church, and it was there I met Manuel.

Manuel was about ten, and he had a confiding manner. I sat on the parapet and found he was with me; he had fair hair, and his blue eyes and quiet smile engaged me searchingly. He had friends, and they joined us, by ones and twos and threes; we became a throng, and I, at the center, could hardly stir for the confidential press. They, not having wine, thought I should have plums, and they brought them by relays, rather hard yellow plums, tough at the center and inclined to sourness.

Though I now had so many junior friends, there was a special nucleus, an inner circle, and Manuel insisted that I learn their names; I know now I shall never forget them. There was Manuel of course, and there was Elidio and Carlos and José Alberto. "Who am I?" Manuel asked again and again. "You are Manuel." "Who is this?" "That is Elidio." And so on, in an insistent repetition. Manuel was a thorough teacher. Elidio, with heavy lids and a thicket of lashes over enormous misty blue eyes, was an able aide.

It did become evident at last that the *festa* was to consolidate. "The procession will be soon," someone told me, and with all the careful courtesy that was appropriate, I disengaged myself from my young friends and went down the road for a short way. I will get up from the road, I thought, up there and sit in the field in the sun until the procession comes. There was a lazy delight in solitude there, in watching the singing grasshoppers and feeling the air's soft touch. People passed on the road below, going up and going down, not lifting their eyes to discover me. So it was for half an hour, and then among those descending were four small and familiar figures. There was Manuel and Elidio, Carlos and José Alberto.

They did not go by undetecting. They were level with me when Manuel, by some prompting of divination, looked up. Their shout was one voice and, like four monkeys, they swarmed the steep tumble from the road. "What is my name?" asked Manuel.

But they were enchanting children, gentle with smiling friendliness. They sought to improve the halting labor of my Portuguese. They set upon me, as it were, a kindly confiding proprietorship. Manuel, soon, excused himself; he returned in ten minutes clutching a gift of faya berries. It was their families, passing on the road, who finally bore them away.

I heard the procession coming, the rather haunting melancholy of the music that *festas* have. They came around the turn of road above, treading slowly and with solemnity, but still with their floating air of happy suspension. They wore the seriousness that was appropriate, but seemed to concentrate on subduing their quiet gaiety. The little girls came first, on either side of the road, in white and pink and blue, with a soft waft of white veil upon their heads. Then there were the adults, many going barefoot on the stones to signify gratitude for personal blessings. They carried candles.

The men, coming soon ranked across the road, wore white vestments over the brushed trimness of their *festa* suits; the foremost carried a high gold cross. Others beside the road had staffs. They carried the figure of the saint high on their shoulders, she and the Infant with crowns, cherubs clustered about her feet. So they came, all of them, going with ritual slowness; and, though this was a religious occasion and they are devout people, there was no heavy sense of doctrine. This was a part, as the rockets were a part, as the smiling dalliance and the little drink stand by the church were a part, of the long blissful passage of the day. Going down before them I met Peter, coming up, and together we went down to the strand where the boats waited under their gay flutter of little flags.

We waited by a Fayal boat, one from Salão; its boat-header was there, rather stiff in his dark suit and collar and tie. He was lean and brown, worried for his boat's paint in the clustering of the people; his mouth was tight, his face severe. As the procession came slowly along the assembled boats, he fretted nervously.

It was evening now; the light was mellow across the bay and an enchantment had come. The crowd about the boats was dense, and, jostling a little, the movement was soft, the voices muted. The music lifted on the light breeze, floating, diluted of its volume, sad-sweet, like something heard in the mind. The sinking light had brought a disembodiment; the procession, coming nearer, appeared to drift. In the serenity of that evening we were a concourse of wraiths.

The procession came slowly to the boat, as if silently, with no sound of feet, only a murmur. In the falling light the cross had become a silhouette; the gauzy white kerchiefs on the heads of the women and girls had a shimmer of luminosity. As the figure of the saint was brought and set athwart before the loggerhead, the rustle of whispers died away. The boatheader stood before it for moments, drawn, tight-lipped; with his spread seamed hands he took the line from the after tub, snubbed it at the loggerhead, and doubling it, set it gently about the shoulders of the saint and tied it lightly. Bending rigidly, he kissed the garment. Then he was speaking, quietly, as if his inward voice was audible.

"Our Lady of San Guia, go with us. Lead us safely. Help

us so that we may find whales. Guard us through the dangers of the hunt. Let your care be over us so that we may come back to our families who wait for us."

Then he was silent, still standing before the saint. Tears were running down his brown sea-seamed face. So, for a time, all of us were silent; then the children were brought, lifted one at a time in the silence to kiss the painted drape of the saint's garment.

Peter and I left now, for this was the last whaleboat, going through the whispering twilight sibilance of the people along the strand. We went up the boat slip by the Spanish water gate, up to that open space between the water and the streets where I had seen the fishing boat receiving its decoration earlier in the day. Now, on its stern, loaves were stacked; it is a custom of the *festa* of *Nossa Senhora da Guia* that when the whaleboats have been blessed, the procession shall

come here to give bread to the poor. We stood among those
gathered there, and it was different from the poignancy on the
dim strand.

The enchantment, the half-real sense of floating, was
there too, but now it was the quiet gentle gaiety that had
flowed through the whole day's easeful course. We talked as
we waited, exchanged greetings, and, just then, I became
conscious of a presence. I found the insistent blue eyes of
Manuel fixing me from below. "What is my name?" he said.

The procession came now, the slow dim phalanx with its
candle flicker, the soft fall and waver of its music on the twi-

light. There were the children and plump barefoot matrons and the sober *festa*-dressed whalemen; and there was the little man in his American clothes, home-returned and treading the stones painfully with unaccustomed soft white feet. They passed, going to the fishing boat, and Peter and I threaded away through the dreaming streets till we came to the church that had its *festa* too. *Nossa Senhora da Guia* comes on the first Sunday in August and, every so many years, that is coincident with another *festa*, that of *Bom Jesus*. And, soon, to this church there came the shadowed trail of the procession, to be joined by another issuing from the church and carrying its figure of the *Bom Jesus*. They merged, the two processions, bearing the figures side by side, melting away in the fall of darkness.

Late that evening, about the time of midnight, I was drawn in the leisured drift of the throng up to the pleasure garden that hangs above the town. Under the acacias and the drape of vine and bougainvillea there was drinking of wine at the little tables and promenading and listening to the aching sweetness of the *fado* singer. The *festa* was nearly done. Tomorrow, near the time of sunrise, the whale rocket would hiss and break.

A NOTE ABOUT THE AUTHOR

BORN in 1907, Bernard Venables has been a writer, journalist, designer, typographer, painter, sculptor, and naturalist. Perhaps best known for his distinctive books on angling, he is also responsible for landing, off Madeira in 1959, the biggest shark ever caught in the northern hemisphere, weighing 1,600 pounds. When not traveling in search of material for his books, he is an avid gardener in a tiny village in Wiltshire, England.

A NOTE ON THE TYPE

THE TEXT of this book is set in Electra, a typeface designed by W(illiam) A(ddison) Dwiggins for the Mergenthaler Linotype Company and first made available in 1935. Electra cannot be classified as either "modern" or "old style." It is not based on any historical model, and hence does not echo any particular period or style of type design. It avoids the extreme contrast between "thick" and "thin" elements that marks most modern faces, and is without eccentricities which catch the eye and interfere with reading. In general, Electra is a simple, readable typeface which attempts to give a feeling of fluidity, power, and speed.

W. A. Dwiggins (1880–1956) was born in Martinsville, Ohio, and studied art in Chicago. In 1904 he moved to Hingham, Massachusetts, where he built a solid reputation as a designer of advertisements and as a calligrapher. He began an association with the Mergenthaler Linotype Company in 1929, and over the next twenty-seven years designed a number of book types of which Metro, Electra, and Caledonia have been used very widely.

This book was composed, printed, and bound by The Book Press Incorporated, Brattleboro, Vermont. Typography and binding design by Kenneth Miyamoto.